The Films of
FRANK CAPRA

by
DONALD C. WILLIS

The Scarecrow Press, Inc.
Metuchen, N.J.   1974

Library of Congress Cataloging in Publication Data

Willis, Donald C
  The films of Frank Capra.

    1. Capra, Frank, 1897-   I. Title.
PN1998.A3C268   791.43'0233'0924 [B]   74-13545
ISBN 0-8108-0765-3

.

In memory of

JAMES AGEE

whose film criticism was one of the
great discoveries of my life

CONTENTS

ACKNOWLEDGMENTS

I would especially like to thank Frank Capra and Chester Sticht, for letting me see prints of several hard-to-find Capra films (including LADY FOR A DAY and the complete IT'S A WONDERFUL LIFE), and for encouraging me. And thanks also to the staff of the Academy of Motion Picture Arts and Sciences library; William Speed of Audio-Visual and Janet Woods and Evelyn Greenwald of SCAN, Los Angeles Public Library; Henry Woods, Don Glut, Mike Aguilar, Walt Lee, Bill Warren, Alan Foster, and Bob Epstein.

INTRODUCTION

I wanted to write on the films of Frank Capra, first, because I found myself thinking of two of those films--IT'S A WONDERFUL LIFE and MEET JOHN DOE--so often that I had rough drafts on them already worked out in my mind; second, because most of the others I had seen were also good, if not quite an obsession with me. That is, though this book could be said to have been written for just two films, it would not have been written if those two had been Capra's only interesting or good ones. The ambitiousness and power of IT'S A WONDERFUL LIFE and MEET JOHN DOE had always fascinated me, and, though none of his other movies were to intrigue me quite as much, I seemed to come across one good, new (to me) Capra after another: STATE OF THE UNION, The STRONG MAN, The BITTER TEA OF GENERAL YEN, LONG PANTS, PLATINUM BLONDE, AMERICAN MADNESS, LADY FOR A DAY. The latter three films convinced me that Capra the director was worth writing about for more than (what I consider) his two key films.

Capra's good early talkies--LADY FOR A DAY, The BITTER TEA OF GENERAL YEN, PLATINUM BLONDE, AMERICAN MADNESS, IT HAPPENED ONE NIGHT--though perhaps, with the exception of LADY FOR A DAY, not as good as the silent Langdon classic, The STRONG MAN, seem fresher and more valuable today, in part because there's nothing quite like them, while The STRONG MAN simply happens to be one of the best of its kind, the comedian-director-gag writer-team silent comedy. These films don't fit comfortably into any categories or genres. They're not much like each other either, except in their wit, feeling, and technical élan. They convinced me that Capra was one of the best, most consistent directors in Hollywood in the Thirties and Forties. It was only in the course of writing and of re-viewing Capras that I had seen long before and all but forgotten that I began to get a picture of a falling-off

1

in quality in the Capra films of the later Thirties (the period of his greatest popular success), a falling-off beginning with MR. DEEDS GOES TO TOWN, centering on LOST HORIZON and YOU CAN'T TAKE IT WITH YOU, and dissolving in the great climactic sequence of MR. SMITH GOES TO WASHING-TON, which sequence I believe marks the beginning of Capra's best period.

I interpret this slump as Capra's initially faltering attempt to assimilate an acute, new, altruistic impulse (which he accounts for, somewhat mystically, in his book) into his highly-refined filmmaking technique. This evolutionary process was perhaps necessary, but it was probably fortunate that Capra's "conversion" occurred fairly well along in his career. A less experienced, less talented director might have disintegrated into mere pamphleteering under the burden of the mission on which Capra found himself, after a strange encounter with a "little faceless man" who convinced Capra that he was the answer to the voice of Hitler. Whoever he was, he convinced Capra that his films had to "say something."

If MR. DEEDS GOES TO TOWN, LOST HORIZON and YOU CAN'T TAKE IT WITH YOU happened to become box-office hits, it's almost entirely due to Capra's technical, sugar-coating skills, to his gift for entertaining, to the fact that those first "message" movies didn't just awkwardly "say something." There is a discernible gap between the entertaining surfaces of MR. DEEDS and YOU CAN'T TAKE IT WITH YOU and their simplistic, preachy cores, and the surfaces were what attracted the public. LOST HORIZON seems to me defective even on the surface, and its success baffles me. It's only with the end of MR. SMITH GOES TO WASHINGTON that the gap between Capra's need to say something and his technical brilliance begins to close, ultimately to produce MEET JOHN DOE and IT'S A WONDER-FUL LIFE, in which message and technique are one, in which the meaning is the whole film, not just a nugget of wisdom to be extracted from it and examined independently or simply ignored.

MR. DEEDS GOES TO TOWN is primarily important as the blueprint for Capra's idealistic-American-hero films,[1] MR. SMITH GOES TO WASHINGTON, MEET JOHN DOE, and IT'S A WONDERFUL LIFE--each, I think, a better film than the one before it. In each succeeding film in the

series, Capra pits idealism squarely against cynicism, and
does it more and more sharply.   In MR. DEEDS, MR.
SMITH, JOHN DOE, and WONDERFUL LIFE, Capra seemed
to be getting progressively closer to what he most wanted
to do and say with film.   The weaknesses of MR. DEEDS
and MR. SMITH can be traced to the simplicity of their
heroes, or rather, to the films' proposition that their heroes'
simplicity is their finest, their distinguishing feature, and
that the betrayal of their trust is a terrible thing (which of
course it is).   But something is missing.   The accent is on
the questionable value of mere artlessness and innocence.
The difference between MR. DEEDS and MR. SMITH, for
the most part middling good movies, is the latter's filibuster
sequence, an endurance test of Smith's honesty and a technical exercise of the highest caliber for Capra.

      One difference between those two films, MR. DEEDS
and MR. SMITH, and MEET JOHN DOE is that in the latter
the accent has shifted, the spotlight is pulled back and up
to encompass the simpleton hero and his exploiters.   There's
almost a fascination with evil in MEET JOHN DOE, with
the people who are pulling the strings--they're not just villains to be knocked down by the hero.   In MR. SMITH and
MR. DEEDS, evil takes an unconvincing back seat to an inadequate, feeble good, which triumphs, unconvincingly.
Evil is triumphant in MEET JOHN DOE: the script is perfectly constructed to climax with the convention and the
humiliating defeat of the "John Doe" brotherhood movement.

      The difference between MEET JOHN DOE and IT'S
A WONDERFUL LIFE is that both good and evil remain at
the end of WONDERFUL LIFE; one doesn't cancel the other
out.   It's not a simple case of good versus evil (despite the
distracting presence of the out-and-out villain Potter on
the side); the forces of good and evil are concentrated in
one character--the hero, George Bailey.   George Bailey
stands on his own as a fully-realized character; he's not
just a model of guilelessness.   As James Agee summarized
the plot, IT'S A WONDERFUL LIFE is "about a local boy
who stays local."[2] WONDERFUL LIFE fills in the Capra
hero's background, which MR. DEEDS, MR. SMITH, and
JOHN DOE left vague at best.   Small-town life, in WONDER-
FUL LIFE, has the warmth and richness Capra's previous
films always suggested it had, and Capra finally gets inside his hero on his hero's home ground.

MEET JOHN DOE - The convention

Frank Capra's greatest talent lay in vivifying tradi-
tional concepts of brotherhood, of the importance of the individual, of the sacredness of life, and at the same time
suggesting why such cherished concepts are inadequate to a
full understanding of life.   MEET JOHN DOE and IT'S A
WONDERFUL LIFE, in particular, recognize both the in-
dispensability and the limitations of such concepts.   Maybe
there's a place and a need for blind yea-saying.   Perhaps,
for instance, the simple affirmations and happy endings of
MR. DEEDS, MR. SMITH, LOST HORIZON, and YOU CAN'T
TAKE IT WITH YOU wield some mysterious power for good,
unconnected with art (which is what I think at least MEET
JOHN DOE, LADY FOR A DAY, and IT'S A WONDERFUL
LIFE and parts of The BITTER TEA OF GENERAL YEN,
The STRONG MAN, and MR. SMITH, among Capra's movies,

IT'S A WONDERFUL LIFE - Donna Reed, James Stewart,
Carl Switzer

are). But whatever positive, beneficial influence they may
have on their audiences, they are dramatically faulty.
There may be conflicts, but they're contrived for easy
happy endings.

What I find so compelling about MEET JOHN DOE
and IT'S A WONDERFUL LIFE is that they take their simple-
minded messages of uplift seriously, but in the larger context of a world which requires more than simple, if helpful, formulas, a world which, in fact, seems to require
the hero's suicide when those formulas fail. They don't, on
the one hand, take their uplifting messages at face value or,
on the other, reject them. There's some play between affirmation and negation. Other movies like MEET JOHN DOE

(e. g., ACE IN THE HOLE, FACE IN THE CROWD), on
the exploitation of the "common people," are purely cynical,
as glibly and efficiently exploiting their subject as their
heroes exploit the people.   They're exhilarating but incom-
plete.   They have a convincing negative but no positive.
Their heroes are just shrewd operators, charlatans, and
the fascination of the films lies almost exclusively in the
audacity of their heroes' machinations.   In MEET JOHN
DOE the hero, Long John Willoughby, and the charlatan,
D. B. Norton, are two different people, and the hero is
both his tool and his victim and is caught up between the
forces of good and evil.   The movie's fascination with evil
doesn't blind it to possibilities for good.   John eventually
comes to share the very ideals that he was helping to exploit, and when those ideals fail him, as George Bailey's
ideals fail him in IT'S A WONDERFUL LIFE, there's
nothing to take their place.   There are ultimately no easy
answers.

        Suicide or withdrawal, in various forms, turns up
again and again in Capra's films as one answer to defeat
and disillusionment.   As early as 1928, in The WAY OF
THE STRONG and SUBMARINE, such themes as noble sacrifice and dispirited resignation appear in Capra's work.
(The plot of SAY IT WITH SABLES, the same year, touches
superficially on suicide.)   In FLIGHT (1929), in a silly,
minor variation on the theme, the hero blows a football
game and decides to join the Marines (the American version
of the Foreign Legion?).   The "bitter tea" of General Yen
was only figurative in the book, in which an aide keeps Yen
from committing suicide.   In the movie (1933), General Yen
loses everything over his love for Megan Davis, without
winning her heart.   His bitter view of life and human nature
confirmed, he takes the poisoned cup of tea.

        With MR. DEEDS GOES TO TOWN (1936) and Capra's
Christ complex, the themes of defeat and withdrawal begin
to assume a central place in his work.   The heroes of MR.
DEEDS, MR. SMITH (1939), MEET JOHN DOE (1941),
IT'S A WONDERFUL LIFE (1946), and STATE OF THE UNION
(1948) are at one point or another torn by feelings of self-
disgust, self-pity, or rejection.   Their ideals fail them,
they fail themselves, or others fail them, and to them such
failure seems like the end.   In MR. DEEDS the hero discovers that the reporter-heroine has been using him for copy
and starts to run away.   Later, when relatives conspire

against him, accusing him of insanity, he refuses to defend himself and assumes, in Raymond Durgnat's phrase, "a suicidal passivity." Only when others rally to his defense does he return to life.

In MR. SMITH GOES TO WASHINGTON, Jefferson Smith and Senator Paine are two versions, one honest, the other corrupt, of the same man, and at the end Paine tries to commit suicide in shame and self-disgust. Earlier, when he finds out that he is simply a tool of business and political interests, the movie's other hero, Smith, disillusioned, is talked out of giving up and returning home by the heroine, who had been a party to the scheme. In MEET JOHN DOE the hero again discovers that the heroine and others have been using him for their own ends. To prove that he was an unwitting accomplice, he must, as he publicly announced he would, commit suicide on Christmas Eve. In IT'S A WONDERFUL LIFE, George Bailey reaches the conclusion that he's worth more dead than alive and decides to kill himself. In STATE OF THE UNION the hero quits the Presidential race rather than continue to compromise himself.

This main theme of Capra's--the longing for life versus the longing for death, or respite from life--is most urgently expressed in IT'S A WONDERFUL LIFE. It doesn't take either easy way out, making its case only for life or only for death. In MR. SMITH GOES TO WASHINGTON, the issues are left hanging, unfinished. In MR. DEEDS GOES TO TOWN, the undercurrents of remorse and self-pity are too heavy for the flimsily-constructed vehicle. MEET JOHN DOE and IT'S A WONDERFUL LIFE are so constructed that suicide at one point seems to be the only answer for the hero. His feelings of bitterness and despair don't seem indulgent or fabricated. Of course, he doesn't jump; in the case of MEET JOHN DOE, the last-minute intercession is simply a tampering with the plot. In the case of IT'S A WONDERFUL LIFE, life is affirmed by the fantasy sequence, which, in effect, allows the hero to commit suicide and come back from the dead: a vision of his friends and his town as if he had never existed convinces him to return to life. This is not a gimmicky compromise. It allows the movie both to isolate the moment in one man's life when there seems to be no very good reason to go on living (and several good reasons not to), and then to give him a cosmic view of his life. It's a time machine that

enables him to grasp the sense of his life in its totality,
not just at that particular moment; and if you think it
exaggerates the mind's power to make such imaginative
leaps, the movie for you ends with George Bailey's suicide.

> ... Mr. Charles Foster Kane ... by the danger-
> ous manner in which he has persistently attacked
> the American tradition of private property, initia-
> tive and opportunity for advancement, is, in fact,
> nothing more or less than a Communist. --Walter
> P. Thatcher, character in the film CITIZEN KANE.

> ... [Charles Foster Kane] is today what he has
> always been and always will be--a Fascist!--
> Speaker, CITIZEN KANE.

Depending on one's political point-of-view and on
what Capra film or films or parts of Capra films one is
talking about, Frank Capra is an advocate of Communism,[3]
fascism,[4] Marxism,[5] populism,[6] conservatism,[7] McCarthy-
ism,[8] New-Dealism,[9] anti-Hooverism,[10] jingoism,[11] socialism,[12] capitalism,[13] middle-of-the-road-ism,[14] democracy,[15]

AMERICAN MADNESS - Pat O'Brien, Walter Huston, Robert
Emmett O'Connor

or individualism. [16] It's no accident that there are so many interpretations of his films: the composite Capra that emerges from those films is almost impossible to pin down politically. I myself think that Capra's films were basically not political, but that they approached politics as possibly holding the answers to the questions they raised, and that this cautious inquisitiveness is responsible for the confusion.

If Capra must be categorized politically, I'd say that, based on his major films, he was apolitical, anti-political, or, based on MEET JOHN DOE, a nihilist. (Surely the Colonel is a nihilist, not a Marxist spokesman, as Mast holds; and he is proven right about society and politics.) Mast finds the ending of MEET JOHN DOE maddening because it's inconclusive; but the point, as Capra writes in his book, was that no conclusions could be drawn, that the movie offered no political solutions. And the "answers" to George Bailey's problems are personal, not political. The protagonist of STATE OF THE UNION finally just drops out of politics rather than conform to its demeaning demands. The protagonists of YOU CAN'T TAKE IT WITH YOU and LOST HORIZON drop out of politics and life. Only Jefferson Smith finds it possible to operate within an existing political system, and, at that, it almost kills him. Only MR. SMITH GOES TO WASHINGTON exonerates a political system.

For all their political frenzy, Capra's films are not really definable in political terms. They were made with a vaguely-defined "public" in mind, not a party or an ideology. They break political "rules" and splice ideologies together. It's not for nothing that they're often called "fantasies": Capra and his writers had visions of Utopia, and not just in LOST HORIZON. And those visions were not possible inside any one, single political system. In MR. DEEDS GOES TO TOWN, Capra and Riskin are not espousing any pre-existing political line when they have Deeds attempt to give his millions away. His act of charity borrows from populism, as defined by Jeffrey Richards in "Frank Capra and the Cinema of Populism," in its individual initiative, and from federalism in its opposition of the populist idea of self-help and the idea of outside help for the individual. Sadoul is in part right in calling it a New Deal idea, and so is Stein in calling it anti-New Deal. But I think Durgnat is all wrong in too-cleverly calling it a Republican compromise, a sneaky anti-New Deal New Deal. It's a synthesis of the

10 The Films of Frank Capra

populist and the Democratic approaches, not a compromise
--the best of both worlds, a Utopian synthesis.   Nothing is
lost.   Deeds' charity is a way of avoiding the necessity of
government intervention and the possibility of bureaucratic
mismanagement, and a sure way to help the poor.   Everything is out in the open; it's too good to be true, unfortunately.   Deeds' giveaway is daydreaming, but adventurous daydreaming, and the movie might have been more interesting
if it had carried its idea of instant, no-strings philanthropy
further and probed its potential.   It's one of those fascinating, "Why couldn't...?" propositions, like the one in
MEET JOHN DOE: "Why couldn't the finest and best in-
stincts of the people be pooled and used to make a better
world?"   MEET JOHN DOE follows its proposition to a
negative end.   MR. DEEDS' speculation stops at the beginning.

Flat socio-political descriptions of Capra's films are
dangerous.   For instance, it's rather dense of Stein to say
that Capra's films "at no point conflict with middle-class
American status quo values...."   The soul of the middle
class is the work ethic and the idea of competition, and
LOST HORIZON eliminates competition, and YOU CAN'T

IT'S A WONDERFUL LIFE - James Stewart and Samuel S.
Hinds

TAKE IT WITH YOU eliminates both work and competition.
(This is not intended as an endorsement of the alternatives
of LOST HORIZON and YOU CAN'T TAKE IT WITH YOU.
Their insipid alternatives are enough to drive one back to
work.)   Capra's films (even his failures) generally display
a deep dissatisfaction with the status quo, a deep dissatisfaction with life.   They say, in effect, that life may or
may not be good, but it could definitely be better.

Stephen Handzo and others have noted that Capra's
later, major films are a recasting of the Gospels, and Capra
himself (never one to be embarrassed by embarrassing ad-
missions) has said: "It sounds sappy, but the underlying
idea of my movies is actually the Sermon on the Mount...."[17]
I'm uneasy with Capra's role of preacher, which is the more
apparent the worse the particular film or scene in the film
is, but he generally didn't reassure his flock with platitudes.
Platitudinizing may mar the surface of most Capra movies,
but Capra's dramatic sense wouldn't let it infect the whole
(though his dramatic sense failed to detect the laxity of
LOST HORIZON, and the platitudes were stranded in the
middle of nothing).   The ideals of brotherhood, happiness,
and true love aren't taken for granted.   They're something
to be struggled for, and won (as in IT'S A WONDERFUL
LIFE) or lost (as in MEET JOHN DOE).   Sometimes they're
too easily realized (as with YOU CAN'T TAKE IT WITH YOU,
LOST HORIZON, or the obviously-wrong, tacked-on ending
of MEET JOHN DOE), but the usually bitter fight the Capra
hero must make to realize them indicates a deep discontent
with things as they are.   Capra's major movies constitute
a search for something better, and find false promises of
a better life in social and political Shangri-La's; in IT'S A
WONDERFUL LIFE, his greatest film, the only real hope
is shown to come from within, which is a thought as fright-
ening as it is solemn and grand.

Notes

1.   It's also important as the first film in which Capra's
      name appears above the title.

2.   The Nation, February 15, 1947.

3.   "Deeds ... decides to give away his $20,000,000 just
      like that ... fortified with a quasi-communistic

plea. "--Variety, April 22, 1936, p. 14.

4. "... John Doe embodied in Gary Cooper a barefoot
    fascist, suspicious of all ideas and all doctrines,
    but believing in the innate conformism of the
    common man. "--Andrew Sarris, The American
    Cinema, 1968, p. 87.

5. "Brennan is the foe of money and the advocate of a
    Chaplinesque rejection of society and civilization
    (he is, perhaps, the film's [MEET JOHN DOE]
    "Marxist" spokesman). "--Gerald Mast, The Comic
    Mind, 1973, p. 262.

6. "Yet Capra and hence Deeds' benevolent boy-scoutism
    ... the gooing sentimentalized greeting card tone
    of the movie generally is banal, 'simpliste,' popu-
    list--on the level of ideas it is absurd, intellec-
    tually vacant. "--Sam Rohdie, "A Structural Analysis
    of MR. DEEDS GOES TO TOWN, " Cinema (British),
    (February 1970), 30.
        "Smith, Deeds, Doe and Co. were universally
    hailed for their jolly libertarian New Dealism; but
    this judgment seems way off base today ... these
    'fantasies of goodwill' ... at no point conflict with
    middle-class American status quo values ... phi-
    listine-populist notions and greeting-card sentiments
    (A New Deal was hardly required--all social and
    political ills would melt if one good John stuck to
    his guns)..."--Elliott Stein, "Capra Counts his
    Oscars, " Sight and Sound (Summer 1972), 162.

7. "Although this class [the middle-class, which Capra
    supposedly represented] must be termed conserva-
    tive in contrast with the left-wing, its ideas were
    confused and uncertain. "--Richard Griffith, The
    Film Till Now, 1967, p. 449.

8. "Capra [in MR. DEEDS GOES TO TOWN] has already
    found his way to the classical scapegoats of Mc-
    Carthyism. "--Raymond Durgnat, The Crazy Mirror,
    1969, p. 126.

9. "... Capra made a genuine PR contribution to the New
    Deal and the new spirit. "--Leif Furhammer and
    Folke Isaksson, Politics and Film, 1971, p. 60.

"Mr. Deeds himself can be seen as a kind of
Roosevelt accused by his opponents of instituting
the New Deal and 'wasting millions' in helping the
poor and unemployed."--Georges Sadoul, Dictionary
of Films, ed. Peter Morris (1972), p. 223.

10. AMERICAN MADNESS "is swell propaganda against
hoarding, frozen assets and other economic evils
which 1932 Hooverism has created."--Variety,
August 9, 1932.

11. "A nation in its movie theatres was being girded for
war [by MR. SMITH GOES TO WASHINGTON], by
the old master of belief [Capra]."--Andrew Berg-
man, We're in the Money, 1971, p. 146.

12. "... [MR. DEEDS'] social theme ... to some people
sounded suspiciously like Socialism."--Martin
Quigley, Jr., and Richard Gertner, Films in
America 1929-1969, 1970, p. 72.
      "... [IT'S A WONDERFUL LIFE] is a very
taking sermon about the feasibility of a kind of
Christian semi-socialism, a society founded on
affection, kindliness, and trust...."--James
Agee, The Nation (February 15, 1947), 193.

13. "[Capra's] new film deal was against crooked capitalism, but was not anti-capitalist."--Furhammer,
op. cit., p. 61.

14. STATE OF THE UNION is "not that bold or revolutionary in tone.... But ... it whips up a lot of excitement for idealism and rectitude in our public
affairs."--Bosley Crowther, New York Times (May
2, 1948).
      "It is sufficiently ambiguous for a New Dealer
hardly to notice, or care, that, on balance, [MR.
DEEDS GOES TO TOWN] is propaganda for a
moderate, concerned, Republican point of view."
--Durgnat, op. cit., pp. 124-125.

15. "There seems to be in his work an unshattered faith
in the simple virtues and their effectiveness in
the long run inside a democracy."--Allen Eyles,
"American Dream," Films and Filming (October
1965), 34.

16.   "IT'S A WONDERFUL LIFE marks Capra's last, great,
         triumphant affirmation of faith in Individualism. "
         --Jeffrey Richards, "Frank Capra and the Cinema
         of Populism, " Cinema (British) (February 1970),
         22-28.

17.   The New Yorker (February 24, 1940), 23.

Notes on the Text

The comments on PLATINUM BLONDE, POCKETFUL
OF MIRACLES, and LONG PANTS were written from notes.
The other, longer analyses were written after an actual
viewing or viewings of the films.   The chapter on MR.
DEEDS GOES TO TOWN is as short as it is, in part because my opinion of it rose slightly between my next-most
recent and most recent viewings, and I had to scrap much
of what I had planned to write.   From this mildly traumatic
experience I might have concluded that the larger the audience for a Capra film, the better it is, except that through
an identical experience with MR. SMITH GOES TO WASH-
INGTON my estimate of that film remained exactly the same.
I conclude that the audience can make a difference with a
Capra film, but does not necessarily do so.   (It definitely
does with AMERICAN MADNESS, which dies for stretches
on a movieola, where it doesn't seem that good or exciting.)

The review of the book Lost Horizon precedes that
of the movie, while the review of the book The Bitter Tea
of General Yen follows the movie's, not out of perversity
but out of a respect for the respective order in which I
happened to read the book and see the movie version.

The first four chapters demanded to be the first four
chapters; the order in the text of the other chapters was
left up to me and is thus arbitrary.

PART I

CAPRA'S AMERICAN HERO

Chapter 1

MR. DEEDS GOES TO TOWN

Columbia. 1936. 115 minutes. (A GENTLEMAN GOES TO TOWN).

Director, Producer: Frank Capra. Screenplay: Robert Riskin, from the story, "Opera Hat," by Clarence Budington Kelland. Photography: Joseph Walker. Musical Director: Howard Jackson. Art Director: Stephen Goosson. Editor: Gene Havlick. Special Effects: E. Roy Davidson. Costumes: Samuel Lange. Assistant Director: C. C. Coleman. Sound: Edward Bernds.

Cast: Gary Cooper (Longfellow Deeds), Jean Arthur (Babe Bennett), Douglass Dumbrille (John Cedar), Lionel Stander (Cornelius Cobb), George Bancroft (MacWade), Raymond Walburn (Walter), H. B. Warner (Judge Walker), Warren Hymer (bodyguard), Wyrley Birch (psychiatrist), John Wray (farmer), Gustav von Seyffertitz (Dr. Frazier), Irving Bacon (Frank), Walter Catlett (Morrow), Franklin Pangborn (tailor), Margaret Matzenauer (Madame Pomponi), Muriel Evans (Theresa), Ruth Donnelly (Mabel Dawson), Spencer Charters (Mal), Emma Dunn (Mrs. Meredith), Arthur Hoyt (Budington), Stanley Andrews (James Cedar), Pierre Watkin (Arthur Cedar), Christian Rub (Swenson), Jameson Thomas (Mr. Semple), Mayo Methot (Mrs. Semple), Russell Hicks (Dr. Malcolm), Edward Le Saint (Dr. Fosdick), Charles Levison [Charles Lane] (Hallor), George Cooper (Bob), Gene Morgan (waiter), Barnett Parker (butler), Margaret Seddon (Jane Faulkner), Margaret McWade (Amy Faulkner), Harry C. Bradley (Anderson), Edward Gargan (second bodyguard), Edwin Maxwell (Douglas), Paul Hurst (first deputy), Paul Porcasi (Italian), George F. Hayes

---

Opposite: MR. DEEDS GOES TO TOWN - Lionel Stander, Gary Cooper, H. B. Warner, Douglass Dumbrille.

(farmers' spokesman), Billy Bevan (cabbie), Bud Flannigan
[Dennis O'Keefe] (reporter), George Meeker (Brookfield),
Dale Van Sickel (lawyer), Charles Wilson (court clerk),
John Picorri and Edward Keane (board members), Bessie
Wade, Jack Mower (reporter), Bess Flowers, James Milli-
can (interne), Harry Holden (guard), Lee Shumway, Flo
Wix, Ann Doran.

     Longfellow Deeds runs a small-town tallow works and
composes greeting-card rhymes for a living. When an
uncle dies, Deeds inherits his fortune of twenty million dol-
lars. He leaves Mandrake Falls for New York, where
creditors assail him. A crooked firm of lawyers offers to
administer his estate. An opera company wants him to subsidize its annual deficit. A girl reporter, Babe Bennett,
gains his confidence in order to write newspaper stories
about him. When Deeds finds out what she's doing, he de-
jectedly decides to return to Mandrake Falls. But as he
is leaving, a stranger bursts into his mansion and threatens
to shoot him. He explains that he is a farmer ruined by
the Depression and was outraged by Deeds' irresponsible
behavior. Deeds stays in New York and begins to subsidize
small farmers by giving each one his own two acres and a
cow. Scheming lawyers and relatives of Deeds have a writ
issued accusing him of insanity. Deeds at first refuses
even to defend himself in court, but Miss Bennett and the
farmers encourage him to defend his actions. He proves
his sanity, and the judges release him.

>   ... it doesn't make sense to have your leading
> man, your <u>hero</u>, Gary Cooper, keep on playing
> the tuba nonchalantly after they tell him he's in-
> herited <u>twenty million dollars</u>! Your hero be-
> comes an idiot.... Heroes must be noble, not
> imbecilic....--Josef von Sternberg to Frank Capra
> (in <u>The Name above the Title</u>)

     Sternberg and Capra were both right--Sternberg for
warning Capra not to undertake such a project and Capra
for thinking he could get away with it. Capra got away
with it, but without quite transcending the limitation of an
idiot-hero. Few movies have encumbered their hero with
as many "Gee"'s, "Gosh"'s, and "Swell"'s as does MR.
DEEDS GOES TO TOWN and survived. MR. DEEDS sur-
vives. Capra succeeded in making a moderately good movie,

but there's more than one anxious moment in it. Longfellow
Deeds' simplicity and common sense, played off against the
big-city phonies, are amusing. He appears so simple to
them that he's baffling. But later, when the movie asks us
to take him seriously, it turns out that he's just as simple
as he appears. He only triumphs by demonstrating that
everyone else is some kind of an idiot too. MR. DEEDS
GOES TO TOWN is a model of writing and directing into and
out of impossible situations.

        A fear of imminent embarrassment, at what the hero
will do or say next, attends the viewer of MR. DEEDS. But
the movie's comic perspective usually circumvents the embarrassment. As long as we see Longfellow Deeds ambigu-
ously--as long as we see that his simplicity is just the thing
to confound the more complicated New Yorkers--the movie
engages. But later, when the director portrays Deeds' simplicity as something noble and intrinsically fine, we recoil.
It's one thing to play plainness off against dishonesty, and
another to enshrine it. Simplicity is a neutral quality. Until he decides to give away his inheritance, Deeds is less a
force--positive or negative--than a charming blank, and because he seems to have no motives--noble or ignoble--he's
a puzzle to the city slickers, who are highly motivated.

        For example, in one scene fairly early in the movie,
Deeds, at the sound of fire engines' sirens, rushes to a
window. Walking away from it, he exclaims appreciatively,
"That was a pip!" Only the context of the scene saves Deeds
from looking like an idiot to the viewer: he has just chal-
lenged the opera company, throwing cold water on their plans
to have him make up their deficit. His action leaves the officers in a distinctly unhilarious mood. And the juxtaposition
of his two actions makes it appear that there's more to him
than meets the eye. He seems to be aware that his audience
won't find his lack of restraint particularly amusing at that
point; or even if Deeds isn't, the viewer is aware that Deeds'
audience is in no mood to make fun of his simple pleasures.

        But MR. DEEDS GOES TO TOWN has a soft core be-
neath its hard, funny surface. Alone with Miss Bennett,
Longfellow asks her, "Why are people so mean to each
other? Why can't they just like each other?" Underneath
that homilies-and-mush exterior, he's homilies and mush.
Understandably, Capra has the actors' backs to the camera--
and it's dark--when Deeds ponders this out loud. But Cooper
and Jean Arthur could be 300 feet from the camera, in a

heavy fog, and the line would still be embarrassing. It's
the kind of sentiment that might be left implied in a movie,
but never stated. This is what is behind his project of sub-
sidizing small farmers. But the more practical, down-to-
earth question--can Deeds give his money away so easily?--
is left hanging and receives an implied Yes at the end. Hard
questions; easy answers.

Deeds is less a character than a set of idiosyncrasies,
devices for comedy and quick characterization. The frail,
schematic plot employs his every action in the first half of
the movie--in the trial, in the prosecution's case for committing him. The trial, in retrospect, seems to have dic-
tated the plot. And Deeds' silent martyrdom is too much
for such a spare plot to support. It's almost morbid the
way it dwells, first, on Miss Bennett's self-disgust at the
way she's exploiting Deeds, then on Deeds' disillusion. Her
disenchantment with her prying reporter role is evident from
the early scene in the restaurant. He's too easy a mark,
and she enjoys being with him. Her disenchantment deepens
until she decides to confess all to Deeds. As with Anthony
P. Kirby in YOU CAN'T TAKE IT WITH YOU, the movie
devotes too much time to her festering self-dissatisfaction,
as if more screen time would make up for more careful development. Miss Arthur, accordingly, spends a lot of time
face averted downward in Gary Cooper's shadow. While
Deeds runs around supplying fuel for the prosecution, all
Miss Bennett can do, as a knowing stoker, is feel guilty.
If she confessed to him right away, there would be no movie.

The above analysis does not, however, account for
the comedy which fringes almost every scene and composes other whole scenes. (With an idiot as hero, a lot of
distancing comedy is needed.) The contrast between Cooper's
slow semi-drawl and Lionel Stander's disbelieving guttural
pronouncements is what, in a foreign film, would be labeled
an "inspired use of sound." (It's an inspired use of sound.)
Jean Arthur's warm reading of Deeds' love sonnet to her
takes much of the embarrassment out of it, but perhaps it
was a good idea to have Deeds flee the scene, upsetting
several garbage cans in the process. The tendency Deeds
has to settle matters with his fists is definitely intended
comically, unlike Smith's like tendency in MR. SMITH GOES
TO WASHINGTON, which just seems uncouth, or crazy. Indeed, probably the finest moment in MR. DEEDS GOES TO
TOWN is Miss Arthur's blissful, encouraging "Oh, I don't
mind" when Deeds intimates that he would "bump some heads

together" if it weren't for her presence.

Many of Deeds' early acts and statements ("Why'd he leave it to me? I don't need it") can be taken either as comedy, surprise, or just plain stupidity, and, much as a critic might hate to admit it, it depends somewhat on how the audience takes them. What's really wrong with MR. DEEDS are later declarations which can be taken only one way. Peel away the comic surface, and there's nothing there.

> With a sometimes too thin structure the players and Frank Capra have contrived to convert DEEDS into fairly sturdy substance ... audience sympathy is confused ... audience credulity becomes strained.--Variety, April 22, 1936, p. 14.

The majority opinion, however, is:

> MR. DEEDS is Capra's finest film ... and that means it is a comedy quite unmatched on the screen.--Graham Greene, Graham Greene on Film, 1972, p. 96.

> Capra's two greatest films--IT HAPPENED ONE NIGHT and DEEDS.....--Andrew Bergman, We're in the Money, 1971, p. 136.

> ... Capra and Riskin ... worked together ... perhape to their greatest philosophical success, on MR. DEEDS.....--Tom Shales, The American Film Heritage, p. 122.

> If MR. DEEDS seems Capra's best film, perhaps it is also because it is the only one with both Gary Cooper and Jean Arthur.--Gerald Mast, The Comic Mind, p. 264.

> What is it peculiar to the medium and Capra, and the genre, that can make the technical and thematic banalities of MR. DEEDS GOES TO TOWN almost irrelevant to the interest, power, classic greatness, sheer entertainment of the movie?--Sam Rohdie, "A Structural Analysis of MR. DEEDS GOES TO TOWN," Cinema (British), February, 1970, p. 30.

In another article in the same issue of <u>Cinema</u>, Jeffrey Richards notes that Longfellow Deeds combines the innocence and determination of Harry Langdon and the common sense of Capra's earlier big-city heroes (without the "veneer of cynicism"), and that Capra's heroines begin to assume the role of big-city cynic.

Chapter 2

MR. SMITH GOES TO WASHINGTON

Columbia. 1939. 125 minutes.

Director, Producer: Frank Capra. Screenplay: Sidney Buchman, from the story, "The Gentleman from Montana," by Lewis R. Foster.[1] Photography: Joseph Walker. Musical Score: Dimitri Tiomkin. Musical Director: Morris Stoloff. Art Director: Lionel Banks. Editors: Gene Havlick, Al Clark. Montage Effects: Slavko Vorkapich. Costumes: Kalloch. Assistant Director: Arthur S. Black. Second Unit Director: Charles Vidor. Technical Adviser: Jim Preston. One of the ten greatest films--Louis Marcorelles, Sight and Sound poll of critics, 1962. One of the ten greatest films--David Wilson, Sight and Sound poll of critics, 1972.

Cast: James Stewart (Jefferson Smith), Jean Arthur (Clarissa Saunders), Claude Rains (Senator Joseph Paine), Edward Arnold (Jim Taylor), Thomas Mitchell (Diz Moore), Harry Carey (President of the Senate), Eugene Pallette (Chick McGann), Guy Kibbee (Gov. Hubert Hopper), Beulah Bondi (Ma Smith), Porter Hall (Sen. Monroe), H. B. Warner (Sen. Agnew, majority leader), Pierre Watkin (Sen. Barnes, minority leader), Charles Lane (Nosey), Astrid Allwyn (Susan Paine), Ruth Donnelly (Emma Hopper), William Demarest (Bill Griffith), Grant Mitchell (Sen. MacPherson); John Russell, Baby Dumpling [Larry Simms], Billy, Delmar, Harry, and Gary Watson (The Hopper boys), H. V. Kaltenborn (broadcaster), Jack Carson (Sweeney), Edmund Cobb (Sen. Gower), Dick Elliott (Carl Cook), Kenneth Carpenter (announcer), Russell Simpson (Allen), Stanley Andrews (Sen. Hodges), Walter Soderling (Sen. Pickett), Frank Jaquet (Sen. Byron), Ferris Taylor (Sen. Carlisle), Carl Stockdale (Sen. Burdette), Alan Bridge (Sen. Dwight), Frederick Burton (Sen. Dearborn), Harry Bailey (Sen. Hammett), Wyndham Standing (Sen. Ashman), Robert Walker (Sen. Holland), Wright Kramer

(Sen. Carlton), Victor Travers (Sen. Grainger), John Ince
(Sen. Fernwick), Sam Ash (Sen. Lancaster), Philo McCullough
(Sen. Albert), Frank O'Connor (Sen. Alfred), Harry Stafford
(Sen. Atwater), Jack Richardon (Sen. Manchester); Helen
Jerome Eddy, Ann Doran, Beatrice Curtis (Paine's secre-
taries), Joe King (Summers), Paul Stanton (Flood), Vera
Lewis (Mrs. Edwards), Dora Clemant (Mrs. McGann), Laura
Treadwell (Mrs. Taylor), Douglas Evans ("Francis Scott
Key"), Allan Cavan (Ragner), Maurice Costello (Diggs),
Lloyd Whitlock (Schultz), Myonne Walsh (Jane Hopper), Ar-
thur Loft (Chief Clerk), Eddie Fetherston (Senate reporter),
Ed Mortimer?; Ed Randolph, Milton Kibbee, Vernon Dent,
Michael Gale, Ed Brewer, Anne Cornwall, James Millican,
Mabel Forrest, Nick Copeland, Dulce Daye (Senate reporters),
Byron Foulger (Hopper's secretary); Frank Puglia, Erville
Alderson, Maurice Cass (handwriting experts), Rev. Neal
Dodd (Senate Chaplain), Louis Jean Heydt (soap-box speaker);
Dub Taylor, William Arnold, George Chandler, Donald Kerr,
Clyde Dilson, William Newell, Gene Morgan, George McKay,
Matt McHugh, Evelyn Knapp, Jack Gardner, Eddie Kane,
Hal Cooke, James McNamara, Jack Egan, Ed Chandler (re-
porters), Frank Austin (inventor), Count Stefenelli and Alex
Novinsky (foreign diplomats), Robert Emmett Kean (editor),
Olaf Hytten (butler), Dickie Jones (page boy), Snowflake
(porter), Arthur Thalasso (doorman), Dave Willock (Senate
guard); Robert Middlemass, Alec Craig, Harry Hayden
(speakers), Wade Boteler (family man), Lloyd Ingraham
(committeeman), Flo Wix (committeewoman), Hank Mann and
Jack Cooper (photographers), George Cooper (waiter), Fran-
ces Gifford, Lorna Gray, Linda Winters [Dorothy Comingore],
Mary Gordon, Bessie Wade, Emma Tansey, Harry Depp,
Gino Corrado (barber), Wilfred Lucas, Lafe McKee (Civil
War veteran), Tommy Bupp, Layne Tom, Jr., Walter Sande,
Harlan Briggs, Dick Fiske, John Dilson, Edward Earle.

        Governor Hopper chooses Jefferson Smith, the idealis-
tic leader of the Boy Rangers, to fill the vacancy left by the
death of one of the state's U.S. Senators. Hopper and pub-
lisher Jim Taylor hope that his naivete will prevent him
from interfering with the deal the state's senior senator,
Joseph Paine, has made with Taylor. Taylor has bought up
the area around Willet Creek in dummy names; Senator
Paine, his protégé, has introduced a deficiency bill by which
the government would buy up the Willet Creek area for the
construction of a dam. Smith's secretary, Saunders, knows
about the deal and prepares for the fireworks when Smith

tells her he plans to turn the Willet Creek area into a boys'
camp. When he brings the matter up on the Senate floor,
Paine departs to confer with Taylor. Later, Saunders, con-
science-stricken, fills Smith in on the details of the crooked
deal.

When Smith refuses to cooperate with Paine and Taylor, Paine, before the Senate, accuses Smith of buying up
the land around Willet Creek himself to re-sell it to the government for his boys' camp. Documents forged with Smith's
name back up Paine's story. To stall a vote that would oust
him from the Senate, Smith begins a filibuster. He tries to
get his side of the story to his home state, but Taylor sup-
presses the efforts of Smith's forces. After haranguing his
fellow senators for almost 24 hours, and after reading angry
letters against him from his constituents, Smith collapses.
A distraught Paine tries to shoot himself and, at the last
minute, rushes out onto the Senate floor and confesses his
crimes.

MR. SMITH GOES TO WASHINGTON, admittedly, is
not so much a movie as it is a pretext for a set-piece--but
one of the most brilliantly sustained, extended set pieces in
American movies. The movie is a supreme example of what
Pauline Kael (intending no endorsement) calls "the Erector
Set approach to movie-making."[2] What distinguishes MR.
SMITH GOES TO WASHINGTON from similar Erector-Set
movies is that Frank Capra knew what he wanted to do with
his set; he knew that it was the movie, and he didn't let a
silly thing like a plot get in its way. He seems to have
taken his inspiration directly from the Senate chamber he
had built rather than from the script (which is just as well,
considering the script).

Unlike the blandly ornate, impractical-looking sets of
LOST HORIZON, the Senate chamber of MR. SMITH GOES
TO WASHINGTON is not there just for (miscalculated) esthetic effect. It's the star of the movie, despite fine, if
fragmented performances by James Stewart, Claude Rains,
Jean Arthur, and Edward Arnold. It's the means by which
Capra brings a rather disorganized, undisciplined movie into
focus. Smith's filibuster in the Senate becomes the center
of the movie, its raison d'être, and critics like Otis Ferguson
may have been put off by it because it was so obviously designed to be the center. But it's the way Capra fulfills the
design that makes it the center.

Capra's Senate is alive as few interiors in movies
have been. It's a unique setting, and Capra and cameraman
Joe Walker take full advantage of the unique possibilities for
staging. For example, in a full shot of the chamber, Smith,
standing at his desk in the last row of senators, holds the
floor. In the same shot, Senator Paine, in the first row,
rises and interrupts Smith. Without turning to face him, he
asks if the senator will yield the floor. Smith refuses, and
his refusal seems an act of insolence directed at the whole
Senate body. The staging of the clash, in one take, with the
senators standing at a distance from each other and facing
the Senate president, generates an unusual, extraordinary
tension. It's an electric, unforgettable moment. And it's a
concise expression of the battle lines drawn for Smith, and
drawn by him, on this odd, formal battlefield, with both
Smith and Paine employing its formality as weapons. Here,
the field's configuration allows the self-conscious Senator
Paine to challenge Smith without having to face him, and the
rules of order allow Smith to ignore the challenge and continue.

Visually, the movie springs to life on the Senate floor.
Capra uses the floor-president's rostrum-gallery-floor circuit, which is vaguely similar to that of a courtroom, to develop a novel three-way routine with Saunders, Smith, and
the president. Saunders signals to Smith; the uncomprehend-
ing Smith gives her away; and the president hides a smile of
tacit approval of his coaching behind his hand. In a variation on this triple-play combination, Saunders predicts the
sudden departures of Sen. Paine (on the floor) and McGann
(in the guests' gallery) when Smith (on the floor) brings up
the subject of Willet Creek. As in PLATINUM BLONDE
Capra at times seems to be playing games with characters
and space, and his technical assurance makes the game exhilarating.

The Senate chamber in MR. SMITH GOES TO WASH-
INGTON, however, isn't just a photogenic setting. It's the
real thing, painstakingly constructed to duplicate the actual
chamber. The desks and railings and halls and sloping
floors have an air of idiosyncratic reality about them that,
while you watch the movie, irresistibly suggests that it was
shot on location, even if you know that it wasn't. Capra
couldn't get the U.S. Senate itself, so he had it built. (A

Opposite: MR. SMITH GOES TO WASHINGTON - Harry
Carey and Jean Arthur.

few years later, for MEET JOHN DOE, he got Wrigley
Field.) MR. SMITH may be pure fantasy, but it's firmly
rooted in a physical reality. Capra's demand for authenticity
was almost fanatical. In his book he writes that he feared
that "even the omission of historic scratches on a desk
might betray the imitation."[3] His fanaticism extended to the
casting of actors to play senators: his senators all seem to
be at least third-term, they look so much a part of the place.

MR. SMITH GOES TO WASHINGTON, however, could
hardly be said to pay dull homage to the original. Capra's
fanatical fidelity, at least to surfaces, is not an end in itself; it's only a springboard. The formality of setting and
procedure acts as a check on the action and creates offbeat,
exciting kinds of stylized verbal duels, as in the aforemen-
tioned scene with Smith and Paine. Political procedures and
red tape, which were just so much verbiage earlier in the
movie, are life-and-death matters in the bravura filibuster
sequence. Points of procedure like the "question," "recess,"
"point of order," "yielding," and "quorum" become dramatic
tools. Capra may not have been exaggerating much when he
told Myles Connolly that he could make an entertaining movie
of the telephone book; he did pretty well with a U.S. government textbook.[4] It's the peculiar achievement of MR. SMITH
that it makes politics, but not patriotism, vital. It doesn't
necessarily make you proud to be an American, but it sure
makes it look as though it would be great to be a senator.[5]

The Capra machine in action during Smith's filibuster
is a marvel of organization. Capra, who usually had trouble
with continuity (he wanted to get so much into his movies),
needed a strong central gimmick, and in MR. SMITH he had
the strongest he would ever have. The stray bits of comedy
that litter the film find a purpose in the filibuster sequence:
the sharp, humorous exchanges between Smith and the senators punctuate it with moments of repose and relief from the
general uproar. Capra masterfully marshals his stars, senators, reporters, pages, guests, and--outside the chamber--
newsboys, politicians, and Taylor strong-arm men, in and
out of scenes and scene fragments. His reputation as a
technical genius probably derives primarily from this one
sequence. Not far into it, the audience is so thoroughly involved that simple changes of scene begin to stir up excitement. The filibuster even manages to subordinate Edward
Arnold's steamroller of a performance.

This streamlining effect has its minor drawbacks.

The Smith-Saunders romance is almost laughably squeezed
into the corners of the filibuster scenes.   But movie ro-
mances come and go, and it's not every day that a director
gets his own Senate.   The Capra express speeds right over
fairly important matters: What exactly does Smith intend to
achieve by filibustering?   How does he think stalling the vote
on the resolution to expel him will help?   (This question is
left unanswered by the film and is somewhat unfairly rendered academic when Sen. Paine confesses all.) Does he
hope to convince his fellow senators of his honesty with his
endurance?   Or is he merely bargaining for time?   Why is
Smith's home-state response so important to him?   How
does he think he can convince his constituents to turn against
Taylor?   But better to get on with the filibuster rather than
stand around trying to justify it.

     Even in such an esthetically intoxicating atmosphere
as the Senate chamber Capra miscalculates some shots.   A
medium, then a close shot of Smith, running out of steam
and words and coming to rest beside a fellow senator, over-
emphasize the action.   James Stewart is one of the most
naturally and economically expressive of American actors;
his face and supple, gangling body tell the story quickly.
Capra sometimes holds the camera closer or longer than
necessary on him, as in the baskets-of-telegrams scene:
the passion is in Stewart's face, and plainly, and an extra
few seconds can't make it any plainer.   And is it supposed
to be a funny or a terrible moment when the pages discard
their Jeff Smith Boy Ranger buttons en masse?   (The way
the scene is shot it's hard to tell.)

     But these are minor qualifications.   Smith's filibuster
is a movie in itself, with comedy, drama, excitement,
suspense, and even action.   (But not much romance.)   Unfortunately, there's another, lesser movie around it.   Some
of the same things that go so right in this roller-coaster-
ride of a sequence go wrong in the movie that precedes (and
closes) it.

     The comic point-of-view wavers.   Though MR. SMITH
GOES TO WASHINGTON is funnier than either MR. DEEDS
GOES TO TOWN or MEET JOHN DOE, the comedy often
seems to be a desperate, confused attempt to check the pa-
triotic sap (Jefferson Smith) who's running free.   Smith's
initially ultra-naive character is sometimes just a butt of
crude comedy; at other times the laughs seem to be intended
to make this implausible character plausible, to suspend our

disbelief.   His gawking at the capitol dome is a good, friendly joke on him, a likable, understandable burst of over-en-
thusiasm.   But his attack on the newspaper reporters and
readers who make fun of him is almost ugly in its craziness,
its unreasonableness.   Is he here the butt of a joke that
went sour, or is this episode not intended comically at all?
(Only one part of it definitely is--the reporter who thinks he
was hit by a portrait of Washington.)

        In MR. DEEDS, the comparable incident, Deeds' at-
tack on the highbrow poets in the restaurant, was more or
less endorsed, by their unprovoked rudeness.   (Anti-intel-
lectualism!   Terrible!)   In MR. SMITH the intentions are
murky since it's Smith's, and not his foes', behavior that
can't be accounted for.   There's no surface rhyme or reason
to the incident, but there is an ulterior motive: it allows
the reporters to begin "enlightening" him.

        Jefferson Smith is just too extreme a character, and
his extremeness is not always justifiable as comic convention.   The film at times either condescends to him or shares
his credulousness.   At its best, the movie remains at a
comfortable comic distance from its hero, as with the capitol dome bit or the moment in the Senate when Smith, introducing his boys'-camp bill, leaps to his feet and nervously
yells, "Mr. President!" (Stewart's leap is startling, beautifully timed, and just exaggerated enough to be hilarious without its being simply too much.)   At its worst, the movie is
downright embarrassing, as in the scene in which Smith
visits the Lincoln Memorial and everyone around him stands
paralyzed with reverence, implicating the director in Smith's
ultra-idealism. [6]   The movie is not just uneven; it's schizo-
phrenic.   It's alternately brilliant and obtuse.

        H. V. Kaltenborn's line in the movie--"What he lacks
in experience, he has in fight"--pretty well sums up the
problems with the central character.   You can divide him in
half, into the little boy lost in the big world and the battler.
As a character, Smith doesn't so much develop as transform
periodically, like a werewolf.   He's a shell.   His involve-
ment with U.S. history is all with the past.   He knows surprisingly little about the present, about the workings of the
Senate; too little for someone who's that involved in our history, who should at least be aware of the past corruption in

---

Opposite: MR. SMITH GOES TO WASHINGTON - end of the
filibuster.

government that history books record. Jefferson Smith's
total ignorance is a contrivance to make his "enlightenment"
just that much more of a shock. Smith is certainly not what
E. M. Forster would call a "round" character, even at the
end, and at the beginning he's no more than a characteristic.
There's the same sketchiness and artificiality about him that
there was about Deeds' skimpy, simple interests.

The character of Smith, the idealist, acquires dimension only in relation to Senator Paine, the compromiser,
senior senator from Smith's state. Otherwise he's a prop,
spectacularly well-employed during the filibuster, but still a
prop. Jeff's mother brings Sen. Paine and Jeff together by
reminding the former that he and her dead husband were
once great friends. Despite the faint, but syrupy, intrusively
identifiable strains of "Oh, Bury Me Not on the Lone Prai-
rie" on the sound track, a later scene between Smith and
Paine, on the train to Washington, evokes a strong sense of
kinship, past and present, between the two.

Echoes and extensions of this scene at two key points
later hint that perhaps Paine should have been the protagonist.
After Paine testifies falsely against Smith before the Privi-
leges and Elections Committee, Smith rises as he is called
to present his case. He stands silently for a moment behind the seated Paine, then abruptly leaves. As Paine says
at one point, Smith is Paine 20 years ago. This sense of
Smith as Paine's conscience is strongest in this scene, in
the precision of the staging and editing, in the hard close
profile shot of Paine, who refuses to acknowledge Smith's
presence behind him.

Near the end, Smith vocalizes his disillusionment and
he savagely lashes out at Paine to his face on the Senate
floor. Smith's violent verbal attack is the final eruption of
conscience for Paine, who shortly thereafter confesses his
guilt. Visually and psychologically, Smith and Paine's pre-
viously indirect, artificially- or naturally-restrained con-
frontations anticipate this dramatic, face-to-face confronta-
tion. This time no self-checks or Senatorial procedures re-
strain Smith.

The Smith-Paine relationship gives MR. SMITH GOES
TO WASHINGTON at least a semblance of continuity. (It's

Opposite: MR. SMITH GOES TO WASHINGTON - James
Stewart confronting Claude Rains.

ironic that a movie with such a weak overall sense of continuity should contain one long sequence whose continuity is
almost miraculous.) It's stronger than the Smith-Saunders
relationship, which, like the Deeds-Bennett one in MR.
DEEDS, is fairly mechanical to begin with, and is finally almost forgotten. Smith passes the ball of idealism to Saunders, who passes it back when Smith needs it most, in a
somber, dimly-lit scene that serves as the lull before the
final storm of activity in the Senate.

Even before the filibuster, MR. SMITH is somewhat
of a talk marathon. Though some of Smith's speeches on
the Senate floor are still sophomoric and preachy, it's a terrific pulpit. Until then, though, Smith, as Otis Ferguson
noted, makes himself fairly ridiculous every time he opens
his mouth. The overriding goal of MR. SMITH seems to be
to see how many words it can cram into one movie. The
opening scenes are clumsiest, with Paine and Taylor exchanging large chunks of exposition, discussing matters they
almost certainly would have settled long before. Capra tries
to gloss over the implausibility of such scenes by zipping
through the dialogue as if he were being paid to direct by the
word. He tries to develop the embarrassingly artificial din-
ner-table revolution of the governor's rabid kids into a slick
verbal routine, but he can't alter the fact that their endorsement of Jeff ("Jeff for senator!") rings false.

The slipshod direction of the early scenes, which are
patched together with words, perfunctory comedy with Guy
Kibbee and Eugene Pallette, and jarring, slightly mismatched
shots, foreshadows the almost outrageous abruptness of the
conclusion. Paine's sudden breakdown is believable--too believable. The response to his confession seems callous.
There's a little too much happy-ending glee over the confession of a man who has just tried to kill himself. Something
seems left undone by leaving him at fade-out in such a humiliating position. Smith is swallowed up in the crowd, and
Saunders is left up in the gallery. And where do the revela-
tions leave Taylor? One explanation for such dereliction of
dramatic clean-up duty is that there were so many loose ends
that Capra and Buchman decided not even to try.[7]

For all the movie's weaknesses in characterization,
dialogue, and structure, James Stewart and Claude Rains are
surprisingly effective as Smith and Paine, respectively.
Stewart partakes a little of the movie's unevenness and the
confusion of his character, but he almost manages to absorb

the unbelievability of Smith into his own personal believa-
bility. Capra says that he cast him for YOU CAN'T TAKE
IT WITH YOU after seeing him in something called NAVY
BLUE AND GOLD. NAVY BLUE AND GOLD is pretty bad,
far more didactic and chauvinistic than MR. SMITH ever is--
the kind of MGM pap in which Robert Young will brazenly
declare that he's out for money and women at Annapolis, and
a shocked Tom Brown will reply, "Gee, I wish you hadn't
said that." And it trusts too much to Stewart's ability to
carry featherweight scenes with his boyish charm. But
Stewart has one big scene, and he's more than up to it. In
it his character defends his father's reputation, and, in the
middle of nothing, Stewart creates a moving scene. He's at
once defensive, unsure of himself, angry, inspired; and he
single-handedly salvages one scene from an otherwise thoroughly dispensable movie. You can see what Capra saw in
him.

This talent of Stewart's for making the most savage
outbursts of emotion believable, even startlingly believable,
went unused in YOU CAN'T TAKE IT WITH YOU. But in
MR. SMITH GOES TO WASHINGTON he and Capra tapped
and developed it. Stewart/Smith begins the filibuster emo-
tionally high, softens and mellows as the energy drains from
him, and returns to high briefly before he faints. Stewart
makes a ringing speech more than just a speech; he almost
makes it a statement of character. Speeches, even in movies, are usually just speeches, but Stewart makes the filibuster in MR. SMITH one of the essential chapters in any
history of Hollywood.

Claude Rains' performance is more subtly modulated,
but his Senator Paine is almost as fervent in its understated
way as Stewart's Smith. Rains gives Paine a haunted look,
as of a man on the brink of suicide or madness. Paine
seems to be keeping too much inside himself to go on much
longer without exploding, which, of course, he eventually does.

Edward Arnold's sleek malevolence as Taylor is about
as showy as it can be without running off with the movie.
There's a scene in which Smith tells Taylor off, and a look
of surprise combined with annoyance involuntarily passes
over Taylor's face and, controlled, leaves it--a moment in
which Arnold makes a quietly stunning, unexpected little extension of the character. His out-and-out villains in Capra's
MR. SMITH and MEET JOHN DOE are actually more intriguing and less easily definable than his supposedly more

complex villain-hero in YOU CAN'T TAKE IT WITH YOU.

The movie's wobbly structure fragments Jean Arthur's scenes so that she seems to be doing lightning-fast sweet-tough transitions in one movie with James Stewart and to be drunk in another with Thomas Mitchell. She's good in both movies, but would have been better in one with Stewart and Mitchell. She can be empathetic and exasperated with Stewart at the same time.

The movie that Mitchell is playing in is perhaps ONLY ANGELS HAVE WINGS or STAGECOACH. Mitchell never had much luck in Capra pictures. He was miscast in POCKET-FUL OF MIRACLES and lost in the plots of MR. SMITH, LOST HORIZON, and IT'S A WONDERFUL LIFE. He did much better with Hawks and Ford. He seems superfluous in MR. SMITH.

Harry Carey, as the President of the Senate, is the calm center of the storm. His benign presence is a reassuring sign of sanity and order, but I think Capra finally begins resorting to a shot of him whenever he's stuck for a transition. The fade-out shot of him after he has junked the gavel is a perfect expression of the dramatic corner into which Capra and Buchman have painted themselves.

> ... it is difficult to believe that Riskin's part was ever very important, for all the familiar qualities are here.... [The filibuster] is among the most exciting sequences the screen has given us.... It is a great film, even though it is not a great story....--Graham Greene, Graham Greene on Film, 1972, pp. 260, 261.

Notes

1. A short-lived television series, "Mr. Smith Goes to Washington," starred Fess Parker as Smith.

2. Going Steady (Boston-Toronto, 1970), p. 121.

3. The Name above the Title (New York, 1971), p. 261.

4. I am probably slighting Sidney Buchman's contribution, but I can't help it if MR. SMITH looks to me more

> like a work of production and direction--stages and staging--than writing.

5. Nota bene: Senators and film critics alike castigated MR. SMITH for misrepresenting the Senate, to its disadvantage or to its advantage depending on whether the castigator in question was a senator or a critic.

6. In his book Capra claims the scene as his idea, taken from an actual incident, which fact, however inspiring, is no excuse since it's Smith's, not Capra's, story, and the tone of the scene is inconsistent with other early scenes.

7. Another explanation: "In MR. SMITH ... the ending which Capra liked most showed the destruction of the political machine opposing Mr. Smith. The audience on which this was tried out failed to react as favorably as one which saw a noncommital conclusion leaving the fate of the political boss in doubt. Capra settled on the latter version."--Geoffrey T. Hellman, "Thinker in Hollywood," The New Yorker (February 24, 1940), p. 24.

> Further elaboration: In the last few pages of the revised final version of the script for MR. SMITH (April 1, 1939), Gov. Hopper assumes credit for finding Smith ("Who went down alone--in the dead of night--and sought out this Lincoln...!") and hopes to ride Smith's popularity into the White House. Taylor is evidently finished. And Smith, riding in an open car in a parade, spies Paine watching from the sidewalk. He jumps out and drags him to the car ("I say it's your parade, sir!") and presents him and Saunders to his mother. Well, it's better than the final revised standard non-ending version. Capra had more trouble with his happy endings....

Chapter 3

MEET JOHN DOE

Warner Brothers. 1941. 125 minutes.[1] (JOHN DOE,
DYNAMITE - British reissue title).

Director, Producer: Frank Capra. Screenplay: Robert
Riskin. Based on treatments of a Richard Connell story
("A Reputation," collected in Apes and Angels) by Jo Swerling
and Robert Presnell titled "The Life and Death of John Doe."
Contributing Writer: Myles Connolly. Photography: George
Barnes. Music: Dimitri Tiomkin. Musical Director: Leo
F. Forbstein. Art Director: Stephen Goosson. Editor:
Daniel Mandell. Production Design: William Cameron Men-
zies. Special Effects: Jack Cosgrove. Montage Effects:
Slavko Vorkapich. Choral Arrangements: Hall Johnson.
Gowns: Natalie Visart. Assistant Director: Arthur S.
Black. Sound: C. A. Riggs.

   Cast: Gary Cooper (Long John Willoughby/"John
Doe"), Barbara Stanwyck (Ann Mitchell), Edward Arnold
(D. B. Norton), Walter Brennan (The Colonel), James
Gleason (Henry Connell), Irving Bacon (Beany), Spring Bying-
ton (Mrs. Mitchell), Rod La Rocque (Ted Sheldon), Regis
Toomey (Bert Hansen), Warren Hymer (Angelface), Sterling
Holloway (Dan), Gene Lockhart (Mayor Lovett), Ann Doran
(Mrs. Hansen), J. Farrell MacDonald (Sourpuss Smithers),
Harry Holman (Mayor Hawkins), Andrew Tombes (Spencer),
Pierre Watkin (Hammett), Stanley Andrews (Weston), Mitchell
Lewis (Bennett), Charles C. Wilson (Charlie Dawson),
Vaughan Glaser (governor); Mike Frankovich, Knox Manning,
Selmer Jackson, John B. Hughes (radio announcers), Al-
drich Bowker (Pop Dwyer), Mrs. Gardner Crane (Mrs. Brew-
ster), Pat Flaherty (Mike), Carlotta Jelm and Tina Thayer
(Ann's sisters), Bennie Bartlett (Red, office boy), Sarah
Edwards (Mrs. Hawkins), Edward Earle (radio M.C.), James
McNamara (sheriff), Emma Tansey (Mrs. Delaney), Frank
Austin (Grubbel), Edward Keane (relief administrator), Lafe

McKee (Mr. Delaney), Edward McWade (Joe, newsman), Guy
Usher (Bixler), Walter Soderling (Barrington), Edmund Cobb
(policeman), Billy Curtis (midget), Johnny Fern (lady midget),
John Hamilton (Jim, governor's associate), William Forrest
(governor's associate), Charles K. French (fired reporter),
Edward Hearn (mayor's secretary), Bess Flowers (newspaper
secretary), The Hall Johnson Choir, Hank Mann (Ed, pho-
tographer), Harry Davenport (ex-owner of Bulletin), Charles
Trowbridge, Garry Owen (sign painter), Gene Morgan, Cyril
Thornton (butler), Paul Everton (G.O.P. man), Forrester
Harvey (bum), Mary Benoit and Mildred Coles (secretaries),
Ed Kane (tycoon), Melvin Lang, Alphonse Martel (foreign
dignitary), Wyndham Standing, Ed Stanley (Democrat), Fred-
erick Vogeding; Isabelle La Mal, Alfred Hall, George Mel-
ford, Henry Roquemore (Chamber of Commerce members),
John Ince (doctor), Gail Newbray (telephone operator), Wedg-
wood Nowell, Evelyn Barlowe, Fritzi Brunette, Lucia Car-
roll, Florence Lawler, E. Dockson, Ethel Gilstrom, Claire
Mead, Mrs. Wilfrid North, Elsa Petersen, Sada Simmons,
Bessie Wade, Lillian West; Earl Bunn, Eddie Cobb, Jack
Cheatham (policemen), Howard Chase, Floyd Criswell, Lew
Davis (electrician), Vernon Dent, Carl Ekberg, Frank Fan-
ning, Eddie Fetherston (reporter), Walter Finden, Jack
Gardner (photographer), Galan Galt, William Gould (sergeant),
Mack Gray, Jay Guedilio, Donald Hall, Kenneth Harlan (pub-
licity man), Jimmy Harrison, Max Hoffman, Frank Jaquet,
Richard Kipling (police commissioner), Charles McAvoy,
Larry McGrath, Joe McGuinn, Tom McGuire; Frank Mere-
dith, Jack Mower, Cliff Saum, Don Turner (guards), James
Millican, Frank Moran, Clark Morgan, Forbes Murray (leg-
islator), George Pembroke, Bob Perry, Ed Peil, Sr., Hal
Price, Stanley Price, Don Roberts, Thomas W. Ross, Ber-
nard Wheeler, Ed Williams, Max Blum, Sidney Bracy, Glen
Cavender, Inez Gay, Bess Meyers, Sally Sage, Lottie Wil-
liams, Ed Graham, Stuart Holmes, Al Lloyd, Paul Panser,
Jack Richardson, Leo White, Tom Wilson, Jack Wise; Su-
zanne Carnahan and Maris Wrixon (autograph hounds), Frank
Mayo (attendant).

        Publisher D. B. Norton buys the newspaper, The Bul-
letin, turns it into The New Bulletin, and fires most of the
old staff. Columnist Ann Mitchell, to save her job, invents
a "John Doe" who, in a letter to The New Bulletin, states
that in protest against the world's injustices he will publicly
commit suicide. With the aid of public and rival-paper
pressure, she convinces her editor, Connell, to back up the

letter with a hired "John Doe, " an ex-bush league pitcher
named Long John Willoughby. His first major assignment is
a radio speech over a Norton station, which he carries out.
But, disillusioned by publicity- and sensation-seekers and uneasy in his role, he returns to his hobo life with his friend,
the Colonel. The speech, however, has a powerful impact
on listeners. John is recognized and mobbed in a small
town and realizes that the message he was paid to deliver
has caught fire with the people. He meets a John Doe Club,
which convinces him to continue as head of the movement.
When John discovers that Norton's promotion is strictly in
his own self-interest, with an eye to the Presidency and a
police state, he is determined to reveal the fraud at the national John Doe Clubs' convention. But before he can explain
his part in the fraud, Norton's men cut the loudspeaker
wires and unleash a horde of newsboys with papers declaring
him the mastermind. To vindicate himself, he decides to
make good that written declaration of suicide. But Ann,
Connell, and some club members stop him and convince him
he can do more for the movement alive.

     MEET JOHN DOE is nothing if not ambitious. It tries
to be two movies at once--a triumphant, uplifting one and a
brutish, defeatist one, and, as in many of Capra's movies,
the attempts at uplift are sometimes strained. Capra and
Riskin's script, which is generally the more effective the
grimmer it is, is at once about organized idealism, about
the manipulation of that organization for fascistic purposes,
and about John Doe, the man in the middle. Far-fetched as
the idea of organizing and harnessing idealism might be, the
movie almost makes such an organized effort believable, at
least within the movie's context of the manipulation of that
effort by other, less idealistic forces. The movie's sounds
and images of idealism are nearly as vivid and imaginative
as its sounds and images of cynicism. And its sensation-
alistic plot elements--packaged brotherhood, suicide-as-a-
stunt, suicide-as-redemption, Madison Avenue fascism--are
a volatile mixture of the wildly cynical and the wildly idealistic. But one half of the movie is nothing without the other
half. Good is inseparable from evil, and a profound good
implies a profound evil. John Doe is openly compared to
Christ in the film ("Well, boys, you can chalk up another
one to the Pontius Pilates"), and the way this movie tells it
is perhaps the only way the story of Christ could be told
excitingly on film, with too-good good ultimately shown to
be a tool of evil.

The film is, I think, almost as impressive in its achievements as in its ambitions. Capra makes more use of 125 minutes of screen time than most directors do of a lifetime's worth of it, and, though MEET JOHN DOE may not have the phenomenal drive or continuity of the long, climactic sequence of MR. SMITH GOES TO WASHINGTON, I think that, overall, it's decidedly better. It's crippled by the failure of one key sequence, by weak continuity, and by one faulty characterization (Ann Mitchell), but it is two-thirds of a great movie (whereas MR. SMITH might be said to be one-third of a great movie).

The two key sequences are the convention and John's encounter in Millville, the town where he is rediscovered, with the first John Doe Club. Each represents one of the complementary forces of the plot at its purest--the convention, the forces of fascism led by D. B. Norton; Millville, the John Doe Clubs. As it happens, the former is a much more convincing demonstration of the forces of oppression than the latter is of the forces of goodwill. But, though these are the movie's key sequences, the failure of one-- Millville--doesn't mean the failure of half the movie.

The ideals of the John Doe movement generally come filtered through a variety of distancing devices, from comedy to skepticism to the presence of the Norton forces. In this one scene only are those ideals nakedly lain out for inspection. It's the most discouraging scene in the movie because it's the most hopeful and also the weakest. It says in effect that the basis of the film is faulty, that idealism cannot be organized, that the "fantasy of goodwill," in Richard Griffith's phrase, is indeed a fantasy, at least on a vast, organizational scale. It says, in effect, exactly the opposite of what it intends to say.

The speaker for the club, Bert, tells John how everyone in his neighborhood suddenly came to know and become friends with everyone else, how even "Sourpuss" Smithers turned out to be okay. And although Norton is as responsible for the club's formation as John--he couldn't have reached them without Norton's help--the sequence plays as if Norton did not exist (even though he's standing there watching), as if this little bud of open-armed humanity would sprout gloriously if left to itself. The scene's effectiveness does not depend so much on your feeling for your fellow man; it is simply a fraud. It presents the John Doe ideal as a _fait accompli_, a given, not as something to which to aspire:

we're all good joes; we just have to let each other know it.
The "bad guys" are all somewhere else--in politics, big
business, etc. It pretends to render the abstract magically
concrete. Most of the rest of the movie acknowledges that
it's not quite that simple.

The scene would be much improved--a different scene,
in fact--if the focus were where it should be, on John. Norton arranges the meeting for John's benefit, to convince him
that there's something to the John Doe idea, but the staging
discounts Norton's influence. (Though he advises Ann, before they go in to see him: "Present it to him as a great
cause for the common man.") The encounter is dominated
not by John or Norton, but by the club, by its message of
the reality of goodwill. It's merely punctuated by shots of
John, interested but understandably uneasy; the Colonel, distinctly uninterested; and Norton and Ann, both interested
more in John's reaction that in the group's presentation.
The latter is admittedly very well-staged, with the awkward-
ness of the situation well-realized in Regis Toomey's self-
conscious, stiff movements as Bert, and in Ann Doran's embarrassed smiles and obvious pride in her husband's bold-
ness. But the group's physical presence is less vivid than
its ulterior significance. They're a living platitude: love
thy neighbor. It's one thing to believe, or to half-believe,
or to wish to believe a platitude, and another to show it as
the answer to unemployment, war, hate, etc.[2] The scene
is perhaps necessary, the convincer for John, something for
him to cling to, but, even so, the emphasis is badly misplaced.

The other key sequence, the convention, lasts only
about eight minutes. Capra doesn't drag it out to justify the
obvious expense. It's shorter than MR. SMITH's filibuster
or the fantasy sequence in IT'S A WONDERFUL LIFE, but
it's just as stirring, and not flawed as they are. It's abrupt
and to the point, and the point is the suddenness of the end
of the John Doe movement. It constitutes the most brutal
rejection of the possibility or practicability of mass idealism
imaginable. In just several minutes it transforms that idealism into disillusionment and scorn and turns the John Does
into a jeering mob. The tomato striking John's forehead
just after, trying to make himself heard without the loud-
speakers, he cries out the phrase, "You're the hope of the
world...!," will probably stand for a long time as the ul-

Opposite: MEET JOHN DOE - the convention (the silent prayer).

timate filmic image of crushed idealism.

The sequence begins with full shots of a stadium
(Wrigley Field, Chicago) overflowing with thousands of members of John Doe Clubs from all over the country.   Its' driz-
zling, and they're singing "Banjo on My Knee" as John rushes in.   Under their umbrellas, they seem to be banded together against natural as well as human hostility.   In fact,
though the sequence marks the end of the John Doe idea, the
communal spirit of the singing and of the silent prayer for
absent John Does around the world is the most unexpectedly
moving expression of harmony and hope in the movie.   But
perhaps it's less the idea of brotherhood than the fact that
this is its moment of truth.   As the idea of Shangri-La
comes alive only when Conway is about to leave it, so the
idea of brotherhood comes alive when it's threatened.   Just
before it's extinguished, the John Doe idea burns brightest,
in the silence of the crowd as it prays, in John's troubled
face as he mechanically mouths the words to "America."

John's exposure of Norton turns into Norton's exposure of John.   Though John admits complicity, his primary
intention is to expose Norton, to keep the movement alive
even if it means sacrificing himself.   He's not like Deeds,
choked with self-pity, sullenly refusing to talk at his trial,
pointlessly souring the movie.   The feelings and emotions involved here--desperation, disappointment, hope, guilt--are
more complex, less arbitrary, less insistent.   It's an enforced silence that ensues.   John might be able to defend
himself, but Norton's troopers cut the p.a. cables and rouse
the crowd into drowning out his voice and throwing things.
The manipulation of the first radio audience for John Doe becomes this uglier manipulation of the throng against him.
When "John Doe" first announces his intention to die, the
people beg him to stay alive.   At their convention, they
demand, in effect, that he die to prove himself, and, sec-
ondarily, to substantiate "John Doe"'s original condemnation
of the world as corrupt.

This last third of MEET JOHN DOE--the convention,
the build-up to it, the aftermath, even the notoriously inconclusive conclusion--makes one of the most exciting motion picture sound tracks.   Capra orchestrates voices, sounds,
and silences--with the voices of Norton and John straining for
dominance--for maximum emotional impact.   Sounds of shock
and discord--Norton's newstrucks screeching to a halt outside
the stadium during the silent prayer, a trooper popping a

conventioneer's balloon--counterbalance and punctuate sounds
of unity and reassurance: the mass singing, John's pleading
for the John Does. The methodical, orderly selling of "John
Doe" to the public suddenly turns into the frantic efforts of
duper and duped to get their differing versions of the sale
to that public. This abrupt change of plans galvanizes the
film, and the sound track is charged with excitement, with
John's enforced silence the dramatic and thematic culmination of movie and sequence.

Ostensibly, MEET JOHN DOE is a movie about neigh-
borliness and community spirit, and Otis Ferguson intelligent-
ly and open-mindedly treated it as such. But his openness
to its positive themes is typical of critics' half-acknowledg-
ments of the themes of Capra's major movies, particularly
of MEET JOHN DOE and IT'S A WONDERFUL LIFE, but
even of MR. DEEDS and MR. SMITH. Stephen Handzo, in
a good, if somewhat glib, summary of Capra's career, also
reacts, less open-mindedly, only to the sweeter half of
JOHN DOE:

> Capra is appealing when extolling vagabondage and
> eccentricity, less so when glorifying plebeian aver-
> ageness in terms akin to a George Wallace rally--
> all the more ironically since his own film shows
> the ulterior exploitability of 'typical' Americanism. [3]

Ferguson and Handzo acknowledge in passing the exploitation
of John Doe, but treat it as if it were a mere afterthought
on Capra and Riskin's part.

In the very first scene, the words, "The Bulletin--
A free press means a free people," are pneumatic-chiselled
off the front of D. B. Norton's newly-acquired newspaper office. In their place appears a plaque reading, "The New
Bulletin--A streamlined newspaper for a streamlined era."
From the beginning, the emphasis is on appearance. Image-
conscious Ann selects John: "Look at that face. They'll believe him." She issues orders to make him presentable to
the public and cannily inspires him to strike a "protesting"
pose for the newspaper photographers by picturing for John
an umpire calling a Willoughby pitch across "the heart of the
plate" a ball. And Norton, aware of Ann's control of the
situation, instructs her to act as go-between for him.

John's radio talk is pure Capracorn (or Riskin ba-
loney), but its content figures in the sequence at the studio

more as a means than an end. (The staging does not dismiss it entirely.) The focus keeps shifting from John to Ann to Connell to the Colonel to the audience. Throughout, the context is of a show staged for the benefit of the studio and listening audiences. The attempts by the radio crew to funnel John's awkward amateurishness into their slick, artificial format gives the sequence a comic edge. He's already being packaged, like a Presidential candidate. The announcer adjusts the mike for him when it capsizes and even replaces his hand on the stem. A prompter periodically darts into the foreground on John's left to encourage applause or to kill it. Both are contemptuous of John's lack of professionalism, but the satirical darts are aimed at them.

Norton is listening to the broadcast at home. At one point, distracted by the applause from the next room amplifying the applause from the radio, Norton goes to investigate and finds his servants clustered around a radio, hooked on "John Doe." Norton has the people in his pocket; the camera emphasizes his mastery of the situation by catching him briefly in close-up gloating over his good fortune as it pans him back to his study. He dominates the scene, and the servants remain in the background, as the Millville Does should have. And Norton's presence dominates the movie.

The script and Gary Cooper, in a performance of surprising range and depth, sensitively develop the character of John Willoughby. He's more intriguing than Capra's other, more famous heroes. For one thing, he isn't saddled with the incredible pristine innocence of Jefferson Smith or the simple, poetic soul of Longfellow Deeds. MR. DEEDS and MR. SMITH do, it's true, disillusion their heroes, but they're so naive that it's easy. And all they can do about it is get mad. JOHN DOE adds an extra twist right at the start, finding it necessary first to provide John with illusions before it can proceed, nastily, to destroy them. As Capra put it: "It was really a much better story than others we told because the story affected the central character."[4]

And John--a Capra hero!--is susceptible to corruption. Though he is nobly motivated--he wants his pitching arm restored--he becomes party to what he realizes is a shady deal.

Opposite: MEET JOHN DOE - Walter Brennan, Irving Bacon, James Gleason, Gary Cooper, Barbara Stanwyck.

The Colonel detects a further noble motivation: "You're stuck on a girl." After Ann informs him that his speech was inspired by her father's writings, he's almost afraid to touch it. He gets into the swing of it and reads on energetically for a while, then finally panics as he senses its increasing earnestness. Capra and Cooper make John's reactions to Ann's speech seem, as they should be, more important than the speech itself.

Even after Millville, he's still not entirely convinced ("A fellow would have to be a mighty fine example himself to go around telling other people how to..."), but under Ann's deciding influence he goes along with the benevolent deception. It's the play between his reluctance and skepticism, his growing conviction (ultimately to the point of contemplating suicide) in the John Doe idea, and his complicating attachment to Ann that make John Willoughby such a fascinating, uncategorizable character.

In the most delicately written scene between John and Ann, he admits that he still can't quite "figure out" the spell that "John Doe" casts over people.[5] It's significant in its linking of the private with the public elements of the plot, a link which most historical and political movies attempt to make and fail to. MEET JOHN DOE makes the connection better than most movies of its kind, in its association of political with personal alliances. (In IT'S A WONDERFUL LIFE, George Bailey comes very close to joining Potter, until he shakes his hand and finds the action revolting.) In this scene, John explicitly equates his attraction to Ann ("loneliness") with the John Does' attraction to "John Doe" and to other John Does, and thus he explains his attraction to "John Doe."

JOHN DOE was apparently conceived and written from John's point-of-view, with the other characters gradually taking shape from their relationship to him, and it was not rewritten closely and carefully enough to eliminate the flaws inherent in this method of construction. From John's point-of-view, the movie is almost flawless.[6] Norton, Connell, and the Colonel were probably fairly easy to fit into the scheme since they're in and out of the story. Ann Mitchell is the only casualty. She's as blatantly manipulated by the script as the John Doe movement is by Norton.

Opposite: MEET JOHN DOE - Edward Arnold, Barbara Stanwyck, Gary Cooper, Walter Brennan.

"John Doe" alive and the film honest. John alive is a fake;
dead, he's a valid protest. But Capra pulls all the theatri-
cal stops to make it appear more honest for John to live
than to die. And damned if the urgency with which he stages
the scene doesn't almost convince you that he's right. Miss
Stanwyck, wracked with fever, almost expires in John's arms.
She clutches blindly at him in order to stop him and to hold
herself up, threatening to go over with him if he jumps. Edward Arnold's very presence, as she notes, is evidence that
there was something to the Doe thing after all. And Regis
Toomey and J. Farrell MacDonald insist that reactivating the
clubs "would be a lot easier" with him. (They're just being
nice, though. The clubs, now without Norton's help, could
use a martyr.)

MEET JOHN DOE - Gary Cooper at the ledge.

It's actually a fine way to end a movie, with tears

and threats and promises and hope--but it's not the best, the
right way to end this movie. This bogus ending illustrates
what an inspired, desperate director can do, even when he
knows there's nothing he can do. Capra at his best was so
good that he could be wrong and yet be right at the same
time. His most ingenious, most devious move is to take his
hero right out of the scene. After Ann appears, he doesn't
say a word. It's as if he had no will of his own, as if the
will of the people around him were his will. He doesn't
have to answer their arguments as he answered Norton's.
His stunned helplessness before their pleading and concern
is moving; but it's also an evasion, a way of relieving John
of the responsibility of redeeming himself. In some ways
Capra's use of the crowd of sympathizers and friends here
is similar to his use of the crowd at the end of IT'S A WON-
DERFUL LIFE. But here the crowd supplants the hero.

        The John Does are not affirming something John Wil-
loughby already knows, as George Bailey's friends affirm his
acceptance of life. They're speaking for him, and he's mute.
It is, I think, a darn good ending: John's appearance on the
roof, at the ledge, is almost as good as his actual suicide.
Almost. He really doesn't have to say a thing. His presence speaks for him. It's an ingenious dramatic compromise,
but it's a compromise nonetheless. It's a good ending, but,
ironically, it's unsatisfying because there's an obviously better ending and because it's the John Doe Club idea that stops
John from jumping, when the idea that he was supposed to
commit suicide on Christmas Eve to protest corruption was
the more compelling one from the beginning.

        Capra has it both ways--a live hero and a live move-
ment. He would have had more if he had had it only one
way--a movement without a hero or a hero without a movement. But he was making movies for a public as well as
for himself, and that public, understandably, wanted its hero.
(Without that public, there wouldn't have been a movie--not
the size of MEET JOHN DOE--in the first place.)

        In his book, in the chapter on MR. SMITH, Capra
says that he personally selected every actor for every part,
down to "five-second" extras, for their visual "rightness"
for the part. If the bit players in each scene of a Capra
picture are "right" for the scene, so too are his stars' performances "right" for every scene and situation. Which is
simply to say that actors did not walk through Capra's films.
Otis Ferguson may be describing Gary Cooper's usual per-

formance when he says that:

> His is the kind of stage presence which needs no
> special lighting or camera magic; he makes an
> entrance by opening a door, and immediately you
> know that someone is in the room. [8]

Critics like Pauline Kael are fond of the early, arguably
more romantic but rather wooden pre-Capra Cooper, and in
films like MOROCCO his presence was well exploited.   But
in MEET JOHN DOE he does more than open doors.   He
fields everything from broad comedy to intimate conversation
to rousing theatrics (the Capra trademark), and in the final
sequence he's even convincingly savage and bitter, before
Barbara Stanwyck melts him back down to Gary Cooper.

Miss Stanwyck covers a lot of dramatic ground too,
and very ably, from genial aggressiveness to idealistic enthusiasm.   She did The LADY EVE (for Preston Sturges)
and BALL OF FIRE (also with Cooper) the same year, 1941,
not long before she left acting and went into her long-running
tough-guy act in westerns and melodramas.   She is, occasionally, forced to compensate for deficiencies in JOHN
DOE's script with pure energy and lung power.

Edward Arnold's powerhouse performance has been
obliquely criticized--by Handzo for one--as limited by the
one-dimensional conception of the character of D. B. Norton,
when one would like to think that such brilliance as his might
help dispel pernicious nonsense about fictional characters'
"depth" and "development"--as if change and growth were the
only way of revealing or presenting character.   (The BITTER
TEA OF GENERAL YEN works a stunning reversal on the
idea of characters as evolving beings.)   Norton is all surface, but his isn't a monotonous surface (as Potter's is in
WONDERFUL LIFE).   He's a villain and only a villain, but
each new scene reveals intriguing new tics.   It's arguably
mostly Arnold's gift for the intimidating motion or tone or
posture, but everything Norton does, no matter how inconsequential, seems repulsive, if only esthetically.   And the
trappings of Norton's villainy--his motorcycle corps drill
team, his troopers, even his whistle and glasses--are as
potent as Hitler's moustache, the swastika, and the goose
step as images of evil.   There's depth in the details of costume and performance, if not in the character itself.

Whether he's introducing his nephew Ted ("All right,

Casanova") to Miss Mitchell, acting as evil matchmaker, or just silently dusting his glasses before talking business with Ann, Norton is crude and repellent, if indefinably so. It's partly his imposing bulk, but it's also the way Arnold doesn't throw it around, as if he knows he doesn't have to show anyone who's boss. Norton's sleek, nonhuman surface is beautifully "developed," and Arnold's memorable performance is in part responsible for the overshadowing of good by evil in the movie. Probing surfaces is another way of seeking the truth.

MEET JOHN DOE - Edward Arnold watching his motorcycle corps drill

MEET JOHN DOE is long, and any dramatic deadwood takes its toll and dilutes it. But Capra and Riskin go ahead and let each actor have his say anyway. Everyone gets to stop the action at one time or another, for better or worse. Though there must be a source of inspiration for the idealism

which weaves in and around the main characters throughout
the film, the dead platitudes of her dead husband which Mrs.
Mitchell (Spring Byington) trots out are more an immediate
source of embarrassment than inspiration.   And Walter
Brennan's Colonel is an indispensable, one-note--abrasive--
character, but his long tirade against the greedy "heelots"
("a lot of heels") doesn't add much to the movie or to the
character of the Colonel, who usually says much less to
much more effect.

>   Pictorially and technically, the picture is a mas-
>   terpiece.--Variety, March 13, 1941.

>   MEET JOHN DOE is a courageous social document,
>   perhaps the most courageous ever attempted on the
>   screen.--Hollywood Reporter, March 13, 1941.

>   [Norton] orders one of his men to reprint John
>   Doe's farewell letter on the front page of his news-
>   paper ... the producer should have let Mr. Arnold
>   remain the villain rather than attempt to clean him
>   up with one line of dialogue.--Harry Evans, Family
>   Circle, April 11, 1941, p. 15. [The producer did.
>   Evans is of course commenting on one of the al-
>   ternate endings.]

>   The one scene which came through all these
>   streamlined Fourth of July exercises with true
>   sincerity and eloquence was Gleason's drunken talk
>   in the bar.... It was just talk, with business, but
>   he made it his, and it will remain one of the mag-
>   nificent scenes in pictures.--Otis Ferguson, The
>   Film Criticism of Otis Ferguson, 1971, p. 351.
>   [Almost every review of the time singled out this
>   scene for praise.]

>   Many times during its overly long two-hour run,
>   MEET JOHN DOE goes so sentimentally soft that
>   Capra has to jerk it back into line with cynical
>   sarcasm or hard reality.... While Frank Capra
>   should be censured for allowing his picture to slip
>   occasionally into maudlinism and foggy, undeveloped
>   ideas ... he also deserves highest praise for his
>   superb craftsmanship which results in outstanding
>   entertainment and for his brave protest against the
>   present state of civilization.--Philip T. Hartung,

Commonweal, March 28, 1941, pp. 575, 576.

[MEET JOHN DOE] delivered its naive utopian message with such fervour, such full-throated enthusiasm, and above all with such dazzling cinematic panache that, watching it, even the most cynical realist must succumb to its enchantment.... Capra's virtuosity astonishes in the scenes of a mass rally in the rain.... --Charles Higham and Joel Greenberg, Hollywood in the Forties, 1970, p. 79.

Notes

1. Some sources say 123; some, 125; some, 135 minutes.

2. The goals of the John Doe movement are not all abstract: members of this one club find jobs for unemployed members. People all over the country are soon going off relief, and the relief administrator exclaims, "If this keeps up, I'll be out of a job." Somehow, the practicality of John Doe-ism taints its higher idealism, by supposing to prove its worth, as if fellowship were only a means to an end.

3. "Under Capracorn," Film Comment, November-December, 1972, p. 12.

4. "One Man-One Film," American Film Institute Center for Advanced Film Studies, Discussion No. 3.

5. The playing of "Begin the Beguine" on the lunchroom juke box is, in the contrast of the song's fluidity with Cooper's disjointed speech, one of the movie's few effective uses of background music. (The less said of the score's simple-minded pastiche of American Favorites, the better.) Another effective use is a borrowing from the last movement of Beethoven's Ninth Symphony to end the film. The introduction to the final script of IT'S A WONDERFUL LIFE suggests the use of the Ninth again: "... which, since its theme is the Brotherhood of Man, might very well form the motif of the overall score, winding up at the end with the choral section of the final movement of the symphony." But Capra evidently had reservations about background music: In the review of the film, by Harry Evans, in Family Circle (April 11, 1941), Evans

calls Capra on his use of "Begin the Beguine," reminding him that when the two met earlier Capra ex-
hibited some reluctance about using mood music.

6. Only once does John ring false; with the phrase "their
own simple little experiences," when he's defending
the John Does to Norton.   At least I would not care
to have my experiences so argued for.   (IT'S AL-
WAYS FAIR WEATHER puts this kind of patronizing
in its place.)

7. In Richard Connell's "A Reputation," the protagonist,
Saunders Rook, does jump (on the Fourth of July),
yet it's an unsatisfactorily easy ending for a too-
clever, smug story about a man who will do anything
for attention.

8. The Film Criticism of Otis Ferguson (Philadelphia,
1971), p. 351.

Chapter 4

IT'S A WONDERFUL LIFE

RKO/Liberty Films. 1946. 129 minutes. (The GREATEST
GIFT - pre-release title).

Director, Producer: Frank Capra. Screenplay: Frances
Goodrich, Albert Hackett, Capra; (uncredited) Michael Wilson. Additional Scenes: Jo Swerling. Based on the story,
"The Greatest Gift," by Philip Van Doren Stern. Photography: Joseph Walker, Joseph Biroc. Musical Score and Direction: Dimitri Tiomkin. Art Director: Jack Okey. Sets:
Emile Kuri. Editor: William Hornbeck. Special Photograph-
ic Effects: Russell A. Cully. Makeup: Gordon Bau. Costumes: Edward Stevenson. Assistant Director: Arthur S.
Black. Sound: Richard Van Hessen, Clem Portman. One
of the ten greatest films--Gianalberto Bendazzi, Sight and
Sound poll of critics, 1972.

Cast: James Stewart (George Bailey), Donna Reed
(Mary Hatch), Henry Travers (Clarence Oddbody), Lionel
Barrymore (Mr. Potter), Gloria Grahame (Violet Bick),
Samuel S. Hinds (Mr. Bailey), Frank Faylen (Ernie), Ward
Bond (Bert), Thomas Mitchell (Uncle Billy), Frank Albertson
(Sam Wainwright), H. B. Warner (Mr. Gower), Todd Karns
(Harry Bailey), Beulah Bondi (Mrs. Bailey), William Ed-
munds (Mr. Martini), Lillian Randolph (Annie), Bobbie An-
derson (George as a boy), Jean Gale (Mary as a girl),
Sheldon Leonard (Nick), Frank Hagney (Potter's bodyguard),
Charles Williams (Cousin Eustace), Mary Treen (Cousin
Tilly), Tom Fadden (tollhouse keeper), Charles Lane (Lester
Reineman, Potter's rent collector), Carl "Alfalfa" Switzer
(Freddie), Sarah Edwards (Mrs. Hatch), Stanley Andrews
(Mr. Welch), Charles Halton (Carter, bank examiner), Vir-
ginia Patton (Ruth Dakin), Jeanine Ann Roose (Vi as a girl),

Opposite: IT'S A WONDERFUL LIFE - Lionel Barrymore,
Frank Hagney, James Stewart.

Karolyn Grimes (Zuzu), Carol Coomes (Janie), Larry Simms
(Pete), Jimmy Hawkins (Tommy), Ray Walker (Joe, luggage
shop), Ellen Corby, Argentina Brunetti (Mrs. Martini), Ron-
nie Ralph (Sam as a boy), Hal Landon (Marty Hatch), Danny
Mummert (Marty as a boy), Georgie Nokes (Harry as a boy),
Edward Kean(e) (Tom, building & loan), Harry Holman (Mr.
Partridge, principal), Bobby Scott (Mickey), Harry Cheshire
(Dr. Campbell), Ed Featherstone (bank teller), J. Farrell
MacDonald (owner of house), Garry Owen (bill poster), Mari-
an Carr (Mrs. Wainwright), Dick Elliott, Edward Clark,
Lane Chandler, Bert Howard, Charles Meakin, Frank Fen-
ton, Ernie Adams, Netta Packer, Beth Beldon, Herbert Hey-
wood, Eric Hansen, Joe Bernard, Tom Coleman, Monya
Andre, Herschel Graham, Irene Mack, Bryn Davis, Michael
Chapin, Buzz Buckley, Cy Schindell, Bert Moorehouse, Carl
Kent, Milton Kibbee, Cedric Stevens, Tom Chatterton, Art
Howard, Frank O'Connor, Sam Flint, Charles Wilson, Effie
Laird, Jean Acker, Phillip Morris, Ed Kane, Wilbur Mack,
Elmira Sessions, Mike Lally, Harry Denny, Sam Ash, Mary
Bayless, Elsa Peterson, Tim O'Brien, Max Wagner, Al
Bridge(s), Frank Parker, Lee Frederick.

Prayers by his Bedford Falls[1] friends for a man,
George Bailey, who is about to kill himself, reach heaven.
Two angels answer them by appointing a third, Clarence,
to be George's guardian angel.[2] Before they dispatch him,
one fills Clarence in on George's background.

In 1919, the boy George saves his brother Harry from
drowning in an icy creek when the shovel he's riding slides
past the safe area at the end of a ski run.[3] A resulting in-
fection leaves George deaf in his left ear.

George is seen next working in a drug store, where
two girls, Mary Hatch and Violet Bick, vie for his attention.
The druggist, Mr. Gower, who has just received news of his
son's death, accidentally gives George capsules of poison for
an emergency delivery. George, not knowing what to do,
takes the box of pills to his father's office. Mr. Bailey,
head of the Bailey Brothers Building and Loan, is in con-
ference with Potter, "the richest and meanest man in the
county," whose consuming goal in life is to destroy the
Building and Loan. Potter insults Bailey. When George
goes to his father's defense, Mr. Bailey rushes him out
without giving him a chance to ask about the pills.[4] Gower
slaps George for not delivering them, but George has him

test them.   Gower, realizing his mistake, thanks George
profusely.

In 1928, George, now a young man, is about to leave
for Europe.[5]   At home, Mr. Bailey sounds out George on
his feelings about taking over the Building and Loan, but
yields to his son's desire to travel.   At his brother's high
school graduation dance, George meets old friends, including
Sam Wainwright, Violet, and Marty and Mary Hatch.   Visibly
impressed with Mary, he takes her away from her dance
partner.   The latter vengefully uses the key to the dance
floor to part it under George and Mary as they dance.   They
fall into the swimming pool beneath and continue dancing.
Everyone joins them in the pool.

Later that night, as George and Mary pass opposite
the old, deserted Granville house on their way home, each
breaks a window in the house and makes a wish.   George
loudly wishes to see the world and build magnificent buildings; Mary wishes silently to herself.   Uncle Billy, Peter
Bailey's brother, drives up with Harry and excitedly tells
George that his father has had a stroke.   Mr. Bailey dies.
George gives up his trip to Europe to save the Building and
Loan from Potter, then gives up college when the board votes
not to sell out to Potter on the condition that George become
executive secretary.   Harry goes away to college in George's
place, promising to take over from George when he gradu-
ates.

Harry returns in 1932, married, and with the promise
of a good job (out-of-town) in his father-in-law's glassworks.
After a family reunion, George dispiritedly goes for a walk
and meets Vi (in scenes cut from most 35-millimeter prints).
He scares her off by suggesting that they "climb Mt. Bedford.... We'll stay up there the whole night...." He half-
intentionally winds up in front of Mary's house.   She invites
him in and tries to interest him romantically.   He unthink-
ingly asks her why she didn't go to New York with her
friends.   One of the latter, Sam Wainwright, calls Mary
from his New York office just as George is leaving.   He
asks to speak to George when Mary mentions his presence.
They listen on the same extension as Sam offers him a job
in "plastics." George and Mary finally embrace, ignoring
Sam's voice.   They marry.[6] But before they can leave on
their honeymoon, a run strikes the bank and the Building and
Loan.   George explains to his depositors that their savings
are tied up in their neighbors' houses and urges them not to

sell their shares to Potter at half their value. Mary saves
the day by offering them what they need, until the bank re-
opens, out of their $2,000 honeymoon fund. She and George
spend their honeymoon in their new home, the Granville
house, and Mary tells him that this was her silent wish that
night. [7] Potter offers George a job with him, and George,
envious of Sam Wainwright's success, almost accepts. But
actually shaking hands with Potter brings him to his senses,
and he turns him down. A montage of George and Mary's
life in Bedford Falls, up to and through World War II, follows. (The wartime footage, with Harry Bailey a Navy hero,
Potter head of the draft board--"1-A...1-A...1-A"--and
George 4-F because of his ear, is cut from most prints.)

On the day before Christmas, 1945, Uncle Billy unknowingly passes $8,000 in Building and Loan funds to Potter.
George searches wildly for the missing money and, distraught, returns home to Mary and the children. (There are
four--two boys and two girls.) He accuses his little daughter
Zuzu's teacher over the phone of causing her to catch cold.
He lashes out at his family and destroys his model bridges
and buildings. He catches himself, apologizes, and leaves.
Potter refuses him a loan and notes that George, with a
$15,000 life insurance policy, is worth more dead than alive.
In a bar George prays for guidance. When Mr. Welch, the
husband of Zuzu's teacher, learns who he is and knocks him
down, George takes that for the answer to his prayer. He
wanders off, and a truck nearly runs him down as he stag-
gers up to a bridge. Before he can jump into the river below, his guardian angel Clarence jumps in, and George in-
stinctively rescues him.

Drying off in the tollhouse, George wishes out loud
that he had never been born, and Clarence takes him up on
it. The cut George received from Mr. Welch's punch heals,
and his hearing is perfect. He drags Clarence along with
him to the bar that he just left. Nick, the bartender, doesn't
seem to know George, and when George approaches Gower,
whom Nick identifies as an old drunk who served time for
poisoning a kid, Gower is terrified by his show of familiarity.
In sequences sometimes cut, George rushes madly through
the town, now called Pottersville and now a gaudy, noisy
place, and sees Vi, a prostitute, arrested. He returns to
his home, dilapidated and cheerless as it was before he and
Mary moved in. At the Bailey Boarding House, his mother,
like Gower, is frightened by his display of familiarity. She
tells him that Uncle Billy is in an insane asylum.

Clarence takes George to a cemetery where Bailey
Park stood, and George finds his brother's tombstone: Harry fell through the ice and drowned at the age of nine.[8]
Mary is an old-maid librarian who runs in panic from George
when he accosts her. Finally, George pleads for an end to
the vision. To his joy he discovers that his lip is bleeding.
He realizes that he's alive again. He rushes through Bedford
Falls and even wishes Potter a Merry Christmas. He's de-
lighted at the prospect of going to jail, but is saved from
prison when his friends and neighbors show up with gifts of
money and Sam Wainwright sends a telegram from London
saying that he'll advance George up to $25,000. George
privately thanks the absent Clarence.

A great tension underlies Frank Capra's IT'S A
WONDERFUL LIFE in its attempt to portray life both honest-
ly and affirmatively. It ends with a resounding affirmation
of life, but its sense of honesty first leads it to a false ending in negation. That honesty is behind the film's final affirmation, too: for the first time since the days of LADY
FOR A DAY, the classic, manic Capra happy ending is the
right way, the only way, to end a Capra movie. The un-
resolved conflicts and inconsistencies--in YOU CAN'T TAKE
IT WITH YOU, MR. SMITH GOES TO WASHINGTON, MEET
JOHN DOE--between the sometimes bland reassurances of
Capra's films and their underlying strains of despair and
defeat seem, in the retrospective light cast by WONDERFUL
LIFE, simply manifestations of a single, all-encompassing
phenomenon--the complexity of life. It's as if Capra finally
came to realize that a natural, honest happy ending is probably the most difficult thing for a work of art to achieve,
that it must be firmly grounded in everything before it; that
the best of life is inextricable from the worst.

Capra, in the film's flashbacks, uses his technical
mastery to establish the relationship of his hero, George
Bailey, to family, friends, and, most memorably, to Mary
Hatch, the girl he eventually marries. This is one of the
most expertly made of movies. In just the first several
scenes, Capra economically yet substantively establishes the
relationships between George and Harry Bailey as boys, between the little girls Mary and Vi, between Mary and George,
Vi and George, George and Mr. Gower, the boy George and
his father, and between the Baileys and Potter; then between
George the young man and his father, between George and
Harry as young men, between the brothers and their mother,
and between George and Mary. Before the movie is very far

IT'S A WONDERFUL LIFE - James Stewart and Donna Reed

along, it's clear that Capra and the writers are after something big: they have compressed material that might constitute a whole movie into an introduction, and yet they haven't
reduced it to throwaway biographical data. The compression
of the introductory material is also an enrichment of it--the
relationships between the characters are developed through
complex scenes.

The best scenes have both a sense of immediacy--of
life being lived--and a sense of the past and the future; a
sense of life both as a particular point in time and as a
whole. The most perfect and, I think, probably the finest,
sequence is the one in which George and Mary wish on the
broken windows of the old Granville house. It's extraordinarily well written and performed; each line, gesture, and
intonation is dreamlike perfection. It glides effortlessly
from incipient eroticism to bright comedy to absurd, lyrical
declarations of youthful ardor:

> What is it you want, Mary? You want the moon?
> Just say the word, and I'll throw a lasso around it
> and pull it down. Then you could swallow it, and
> it'd all dissolve, see, and the moonbeams would
> shoot out of your fingers and your toes, and the
> ends of your hair....

The movie is open to and aware of so much of life
that it constantly surprises, as it does here, by extending
itself further just when it seems to have reached its limits.
This sequence is alive to the past, the present, and the future of George Bailey and Mary Hatch; their lives are compressed into this one sequence. The transient and the eternal seem one, or two ways of expressing the same idea.
George and Mary's mutual attraction and their dreams for
the future seem in harmony.

The harmony is shattered by the news of Mr. Bailey's
stroke. But the last shot of the sequence is not of the car
as it takes George away to his father. It's rather a five-
second close shot of Mary, with little expression (or no expression) in her face, as she watches the car drive off.
One could read concern, disappointment, or sadness into it,
but just the fact of the shot is more important than any expression that may be in Mary's face.

Mary is the link to the future for George, from her
first scene at the soda fountain when she bends over the

counter and whispers, "George Bailey, I'll love you till the
day I die," intentionally into George's bad ear. (As far as
I'm concerned, Capra could have justified the whole movie
with that line.) Her window-wish is to live with George
someday in the Granville house. She's the constant in
George's life after his father dies. And the brief, Mona
Lisa shot of Mary that ends this sequence is the movie's
most beautiful expression of this sense of her fixed presence
in his life. It echoes two other, similar shots of Mary elsewhere in the film. Earlier, the girl Mary, sitting on a
soda fountain stool, watches George dash off to consult his
father. Later, Mary looks out the rain-streaked cab window
after George as he interrupts their honeymoon to stop the
run on the Building and Loan. Even in the excitement of the
moment the film doesn't lose sight of her and all that she
implies: patience, endurance, hope. The burst of music
that accompanies the five-second shot of Mary is not really
expressive of anything definite either. But its simple acknowledgment of the significance of the shot is sufficient; it
effectively marks for me one of the most moving single shots
on film.

An irony implicit through most of the movie, and ack-
nowledged at the end, is that the town George so desperately
wants to escape from offers him a fuller life than probably
any he could find elsewhere. He has a family (whether it's,
earlier, Peter Bailey's or, later, George Bailey's), friends,
a girl (or, later, a wife), and a rewarding job. But, though
he may love Bedford Falls, he hates the fact that his conscience and sense of responsibility force him to remain there.
Capra, Goodrich, Hackett, and Swerling make George Bailey
at once one of the luckiest and one of the unluckiest people
on earth, and it's this irony that makes a whole-heartedly
happy ending possible, as it also makes possible the earlier,
false ending, the one emphasizing his unluckiness, the other
his luckiness. Such an equilibrium is easily upset, and it's
not surprising that a critic like William S. Pechter (referring
to Capra's films in general) might see in the movie only
"... the frustration and aridity of small-town American life."[9]

If you see George's wife, children, job, and friends,
as he in his desperation sees them, as only so many obligations for George, then IT'S A WONDERFUL LIFE is truly
arid. But the film sees them as both obligations and fulfill-
ment for George.[10] George's life takes on meaning both
from his relationships with others and from his private
dreams of escape and adventure. In fact, such is the power

of Capra's idealization of Mary Hatch, and the power of a
beautiful face (Donna Reed's), that the balance would seem
to me to be more easily tipped in favor of George Bailey and
Bedford Falls.   The image of Mary that's presented to George
and to us at the dance is not one we're likely to forget.
That image and the movie's other images (in the Bailey
household, at the dance, in the drugstore, in the Granville
house) of the richness of small-town life make "arid" a totally inappropriate adjective for the movie.

Although George apparently leads a rich, full life, the
movie keeps you acutely aware that it's not the life he intended to lead. [11]   Through editing, camera movement, the
movement of actors, and the use of sound, Capra keeps the
private as well as the public George Bailey in focus.   The
movie fluently and unobtrusively isolates George--within busy,
noisy scenes--in order to probe his mental and emotional
state, in effect to fix his consciousness at key points in the
narrative.   These fixes function as soliloquies, visually suggesting through context rather than verbally presenting
George's thoughts and feelings.   When George meets Harry
and his bride Ruth at the train station, he's a full participant
in the proceedings until Ruth lets slip that her father has offered Harry a job, a job that would take Harry away from
Bedford Falls and leave George back at the Building and Loan.
George suddenly falls silent, Harry returns to the train for
his luggage, and the scene has turned from one of George in
the context of a group into one of George isolated by a medium close shot.   Aurally, however, he's still in a context of
excited voices; and that context emphasizes his silence.   The
aural contrast, the visual isolation, and the look on George's
face pointedly convey his discouragement, and the moment
seems to be suspended in time.

Much later in the film, Capra similarly expresses
George's psychological and emotional isolation when, in a
close shot, George, who is faced with scandal and prison,
hugs his son to himself as his daughter, Janie, offscreen,
continues to play "Hark! the Herald Angels Sing" on the family piano.   A medium, then a close shot of Mary as, dec-
orating the Christmas tree, she happens to notice George's
private display of emotion, movingly bridges the gap between
the sense of family unity and George's self-absorption.

In the scene following the one at the station, after a
family photograph before the Bailey home, all but George
and Uncle Billy file inside to continue the family reunion.

At the station, before Ruth's bombshell, George had told
Billy that the "three most exciting sounds in the world" were
"anchor chains, plane motors, and train whistles." Billy
soon wanders off down the street, leaving George alone on
the front porch. Through the screen door, he notices his
mother, Harry, and Ruth getting acquainted. He paces
around the walk a bit and, at the sound of a train whistle,
abruptly looks up.

This eloquent juxtaposition of images prefaces the
scene at Mary's, which is a culmination of the main themes
of the movie's first half--George's wish to quit Bedford Falls,
Mary's patient love, George's placing of the Building and
Loan above financial success and travel. The prefatory im-
agery helps to explain why every move that Mary makes is
wrong. She can't please George since he sees her, as the
scene develops it, as part of a three-part equation: Mary/
marriage = Building and Loan = job in plastics. To succumb to one is to succumb to the other two (i.e., to give
up his dreams for good). All three remind him that, liter-
ally and figuratively, he's going nowhere. Mary's unfortunate,
"Nice about your brother Harry and Ruth, isn't it?", which
she intends as an exploratory paean to marriage, means
"back to the Building and Loan" to him. His discontent becomes hers and, after he leaves, she smashes the record
of "Buffalo Gals" which she was playing for him. His dreams
have faded; her perfect patience is finally exhausted.

In the second half of the sequence, after George returns for his hat, the intensity of Mary's presence--the intensity of their undeclared love for each other--overcomes
his resistance to her as a reminder of his stagnated life.
The movie's sense of life, both as of the moment and as a
continuity, is at its strongest here, with the whole of George's
and Mary's lives--everything they have been, everything they
will be--seemingly depending on this particular moment.[12]

Josef von Sternberg, in The SALVATION HUNTERS,
analyzed the destructiveness of the life of a dreamer to those
he loved. In IT'S A WONDERFUL LIFE, Frank Capra ex-
amines the frustrated dreamer's vein of self-destructiveness.
It's not just his financial crisis or a vague, lingering discontent that leads George Bailey on to suicide, but a state
of mind, induced by that crisis and discontent. His discontent with life suddenly crystallizes and leaves him in a psychological state in which he prefers discontent. It's not only
events, but events aided by George's imagination that drive

IT'S A WONDERFUL LIFE - Donna Reed and James Stewart

him to the brink of suicide.   Things don't just happen to him.
He aggravates the situation that he finds himself in with a
despairing anger.   Life kicks him, and he kicks it back,
making it so much the worse for him.   He presumes he's
finished in business, so he suicidally begins severing his last
ties with life--with his family, with God.   When he lashes
out at Billy and at his wife and children, he's not working
off his anger; he's deepening it into something more perma-
nent, final.   He's writing his own end.   He's trying to make
his life neat and orderly, uncomplicatedly bleak.

Even as George nears suicide, however, the movie
keeps an eye open to life.   The sequence of events leading
up to the climactic sequence is not one of unchecked bleak-
ness, as is that latter sequence.   George's visit to his little
girl Zuzu's sickbed has a special sense of tenderness and
sadness to it.   As Martini has Welch, Zuzu's teacher's husband, tossed out of his bar, he exclaims, "You hit my best
friend!"   George is nevertheless convinced that his suicide
is best for everyone, that his personal feeling of powerlessness coincides with an actual uselessness to others.   His
despair takes, in part, a deluded form of concern for others,
a form which is a logical extension both of his lifelong selflessness and of his frustration.

The fantasy sequence is the most important sequence,
the one that bridges the movie's dual endings and gives added
dimension to every other sequence.   It's like the trial in
MR. DEEDS GOES TO TOWN in that it echoes all that comes
before it; unlike it in that everything before it doesn't seem
to exist only for it.   Fantasy in IT'S A WONDERFUL LIFE
is the means for a return to life rather than, as in LOST
HORIZON, an escape from it.   William S. Pechter says that,
for him, the film ends on the bridge in "a sense of utter
isolation, final despair...."13   But what does the following
sequence do but compound George Bailey's sense of isolation
and, in so doing, transform his longing for death into longing
for life?

In the original story, "The Greatest Gift," by Philip
Van Doren Stern, the angel Clarence gives the hero, George
Pratt, a satchel so that he can pose as a salesman and thus,
as a stranger in a world into which he was never born, approach people in their homes.   He discreetly visits his parents and his wife and talks to them without causing a scene.
The satchel makes the story "reasonable" and dry.   It effectively drains all the emotion out of the subject.14   George

Pratt's absence from the world adversely affects the lives of
several people, and he witnesses the changes. That's all
there is to it.

     The movie discards the satchel. The master stroke
of the climactic fantasy sequence is that George Bailey is
actively involved in it. He's not a detached observer. He
begins it by setting out for the bar that he just left, as if
he could return to his normal life. It's not clear to him
that he's supposed to be a silent witness of the changes in
the town and its inhabitants. It's his confusion, the fact that
he doesn't get the point right away, that makes these nightmare scenes so affecting.[15] Clarence can't convince George
that he does not exist. He has to find out for himself.

     When George accosts Gower, the latter recoils. To
him George is a stranger; to George, Gower's reaction to
him is inexplicable (since he doesn't accept Clarence's explanation), and this inexplicability makes Gower's actions
terrifying to him. George refuses to believe that Bert and
Ernie, the cab driver, don't know him. (When he's restored
to life, he asks Bert, the first person he encounters, "Do
you know me?") He thinks he's having a bad dream or that
Clarence has hypnotized him or that it's just "some bad liq-
uor or something." His fear begins to deepen when his
mother says she doesn't recognize him and he can't do anything about it. The most harrowing episode is the one at
the cemetery where Bailey Park should be, in the desolation
of the setting, in the finality of the inscription on the tombstone ("In Memory of Our Beloved Son - Harry Bailey -
1911-1919"), in the madness of George's rejection of it.

     George's violent refusal to accept his "death" is, in
a way, already an acceptance of life even at the beginning of
the sequence. But what finally moves him to plead to be
restored to life is a sense of not belonging, anywhere, to
anyone; an exaggerated, absolute sense of what one can feel
in life, an extension of feelings of alienation, loneliness, and
rootlessness. At some point in one's life the difference between absolute and relative powerlessness might not seem to
matter. The intention of IT'S A WONDERFUL LIFE is to
make the difference matter.

     James Agee was right to call the film on its implica-
tion, strongest in the fantasy sequence, that "whether people
turn out well or ill depends overwhelmingly on outside circumstances."[16] I think the presence of that implication is

due in part to Capra's esthetic shortcutting and use (both
valid and invalid) of hyperbole. Capra liked to make his
points with crowds, and the only way to end this movie with
a crowd was to have George Bailey's life affect everyone
within 20 miles of Bedford Falls. Even allowing for hyperbole, it's not altogether reasonable that the presence or absence of one person, chosen at random at least, would alter
so many people's lives so radically. It's one thing for
George to mean something to so many and another for him
to mean everything.

The implication that Agee detected in the movie, however, is also I think very much intended and not just an accident of hyperbole. As late as 1961 Capra was still saying
(this time of POCKETFUL OF MIRACLES), "This film dram-
atizes the power of a kind act."[17] I think that he's certainly right in holding that good tends to generate good, and bad,
bad; but they don't necessarily. In the case of George Bailey
and his single-handed liberation from Potter of Bedford Falls,
Capra oversimplifies tendencies into necessities--at least
when one looks at the movie from the viewpoint of George's
friends and relatives. From their viewpoint, it amounts almost to a tract on predestination. They're either saved by
George in the flashbacks or damned by Potter in the dream
sequence. Seen from the right--or rather, wrong--angle,
the film denies the free will of the individual.

The movie, by making the impact of George's life on
others so obvious, so extreme, risks being misinterpreted
in the manner that Pauline Kael found "prissy liberals" mis-
interpreting IKIRU:

> ... the message they take out of IKIRU ... [is]
> not that one man did manage to triumph over
> bureaucracy but that the meaning of life is in do-
> ing a bit of goody good good for others.[18]

But the point the film--in particular, the fantasy sequence--
makes most dramatically is that these people to whom
George's selflessness means so much mean just as much to
him. He's life to them, and they're life to him.

In the dream sequence, the dramatic focus is on
George, on his attempts to communicate to others, and not
on the changes so glaringly apparent in them and in the town.
Only once or twice is the focus blurred. That his brother
Harry died because George was not there to save him or

that another boy died because George was not there to stop
Gower is one thing, a matter of George's being in the right
place at the right time. But Mary's becoming an old maid
because George wasn't there to marry her is another matter
entirely. (In the original story, Mary more credibly marries someone else. George Pratt would have made a more
ideal husband.) It's one of those radical-romantic notions
(inherent in such other fantasies as PORTRAIT OF JENNIE
and PETER IBBETSON) of love and predestination--the tanta-
lizingly eerie thought that one has only one chance for ful-
fillment through love.

        The movie presents George as the focus of Mary's
life, but the idea of George as its only possible focus is beyond even this movie's scope. To make Mary's spinsterhood
credible it would have to stop, go back, and present her
whole life without George, as well as her life with him. As
it is, the leap from Mary the radiant young woman to Mary
the old maid leaves too much to the imagination. And it
doesn't help that Mary's appearance--unsightly glasses, hair
tied back tightly, frightened bird-like movements--is a trifle
severe: instant old maid.[19] Capra's talent for making
points quickly, visually, backfires here. Ironically, the person who figured most memorably in George's life is the one
unbelievable part of his vision. The lack of a convincing
image of Mary is the sequence's, the movie's, one great
disappointment.

        In a sense, the changes in Nick and Vi are as objec-
tionable as the change in Mary. Without George's aid and
friendship, they automatically turned bad. But as presented,
these changes are not instantly rejectable. It's the sudden
severity of Mary that's ruinous. It's as if her life-long attraction to George were responsible for her character rather
than part of it. Most of the other transformations can be
linked directly or indirectly to events affected by George's
presence or absence rather than to attitudes--for instance,
the death of Mrs. Bailey's only child, which might scar her
life.

        The way the movie actually employs this idea of af-
fecting, however, turns the "You'll be sorry when I'm gone"
suicidal attitude back on itself. George is gone, but he's
the one who's sorry. He's the one who sees, who feels, the
differences his absence makes in others and in himself. If,
philosophically, the sequence is questionable, psychologically
it's brilliant. It takes all the good arguments for suicide

and, by carrying them to their logical extremes, turns them
into better arguments against it.

The angels' delegation of Clarence to be George's
guide through Pottersville proves a very mixed blessing for
the audience.   Agee, I think, was a shade too vitriolic about
him, taking him a bit further than he was meant to be taken
or validly can be taken, finding in him evidence of a kind of
"heresy and of deceit of the soul." Clarence is really an
esthetic, not a spiritual fraud.   He's a conventionally-lovable,
conventionally-dumb character, though Henry Travers does
bring something extra to his naivete and child-like nature.

Clarence, however, is indispensable in a way: his
presence, which eases George into the dream sequence, inspires some of the sharpest writing and playing in the movie.
His running gag about getting his wings is low-grade, "B"-
movie-angel whimsy, an embarrassment to the film.   But
for the distancing comedy aimed at wearing down initial audience resistance to this cherub and to the fantasy elements in
the script, the writers came up with one good line after another.   It's the several believable attitudes taken towards
Clarence's declaration of himself as a 292-year-old angel
that account for this consistency of invention: comic incre-
dulity (Tom Fadden's double takes are too broad, but the collapsing chair is perfectly timed), belligerent impatience (a
comic gem of a performance from Sheldon Leonard), and
humoring indulgence and mock-dismay (Stewart: "Well, you
look like about the kind of an angel I'd get").

Though, technically, most of the movie is on the level
of wizardry, Capra does, occasionally, as with the unlikely
apparition of Mary, misjudge or misuse his technical facility
for heightening or softening emotion.   He shoots the first
scene between George and Mr. Gower in impersonal medium
shots, through racks of chemicals, but it's still too strong,
and it's too early in the movie to set off such violent emotions.   Even Capra can't contain the volatile maudlin quality
of the situation.   In the middle of the fantasy sequence, he
has a frightened George run up to the camera (after his
mother has shut him out) into extreme close-up and very
slowly and deliberately turn his head.   This moment may be
a necessary step in the process of his illumination, but the
shot looks silly in its exaggeration of George's features,

Opposite: IT'S A WONDERFUL LIFE - Henry Travers, Tom
Fadden, James Stewart.

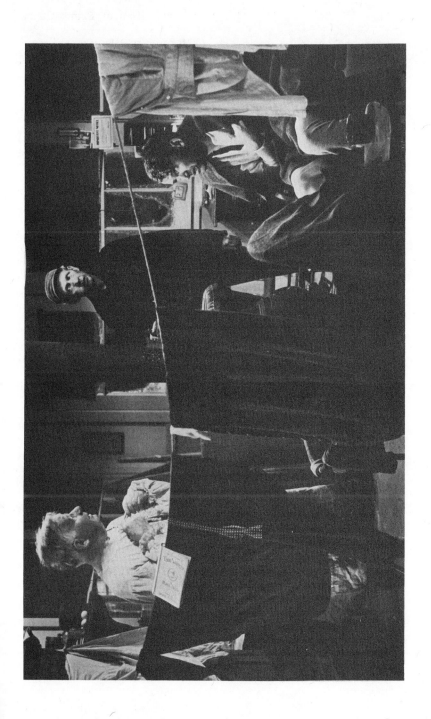

even broken up by an insert of Clarence. It's like an over-
explicit, textbook illustration of the cliché, "The full horror
of the situation suddenly dawned on him."

These examples, though, are the exceptions. Capra
is generally in complete control of his material and perfectly
judges most individual shots, in terms of duration, distance
between subject and camera, and context (within other shots),
for emotional weight--as, for instance, with an earlier, similar close-up of George which catches him as he is about to
leave the Building and Loan and which vividly punctuates the
scene with his realization that his departure would mean the
end of the organization.

I don't find the movie's happy ending--the vision's conversion of George from despair to joy--at all contrived. If
a trace of arbitrariness taints it, though, it mirrors life, in
which one's attitude towards life can change from moment to
moment, on the basis of perhaps nothing but a stray thought.
If you want to, you can interpret the vision as just that,
George's feverish reexamination of his life as he stands on
the bridge. IT'S A WONDERFUL LIFE resembles Tolstoy's
Anna Karenina (which Capra had read and admired and at
least twice considered filming) in that it moves from the suicide of a protagonist to affirmation. In place of the dual
ending and the deux ex machina, Anna Karenina has its dual
protagonists, Anna and Levin.

To preserve what he considers the whole of WONDER-
FUL LIFE, William S. Pechter dismisses the ending: "...
the film ends, in effect, with the hero's suicide."[20] (Critics
have tried to separate the (inseparable) halves of Anna Karenina too, perhaps finding its universe-embracing ending a bit
"extreme.") He calls the movie an accidental masterpiece:
"Capra's desperation is his final honesty. It ruthlessly ex-
poses his own affirmation as pretense...."[21] I think Pechter
is overreacting to the usual, half-truth conceptions of Capra
as a champion of noisy optimism, to which conceptions his
movies principally conform in that their mixtures of optimism
and pessimism almost invariably end on the optimistic note.
He's right to call attention to the earlier, false ending of
despair, but not to draw it away from the actual ending.
Capra's honesty lies not in unyielding despair or simple affirmation, but in the necessarily uneasy alliance of despair
and affirmation.[22] The movie is an argument for life because it's a whole picture of life. It's an uncompromising
vision of life as heaven and hell; it depicts extremes of hap-

piness and unhappiness.   If the movie assumes anything about
life, it's that it must be argued for, not that it's wonderful
or terrible.

Though the ending itself isn't flawed, it is, perhaps,
unnecessarily ecstatic.   A quiet family reunion would have
been perfect, but the noisy throng does reinforce the movie's
idea of life-as-friendship, going as it does beyond a simple
cast re-gathering.   The conclusion constitutes the movie's
second family reunion, and the movie is based on the idea
of reunion.   The handshake, the kiss, the spoken or unspoken
greeting are motifs, from George and Harry's slightly foolish
exchange of "Old Professor Phi Beta Kappa All-American
Bailey"'s and "Old George Geographic Explorer Bailey"'s at
the station, to the magical series of looks and smiles George
and Mary exchange over a crowded dance floor, to Mary's
"Welcome home, Mr. Bailey" to George in their honeymoon
house.   Meetings and reunions, like the ending, mark and
celebrate changes and growth in the characters.   They give
the movie a strong sense of time passing and people changing
and adjusting to each other's changes.

But the double miracle--the money's coming so close
upon George's second gift of life--is a bit too much.   Most
of the movie is just right.   Some of it is too much.   None
of it is too little.   Agee called some of its vitality "cooked-
up and applied rather than innate," such as the opening of
the dance floor, and Capra's determination to bring every
scene vividly to life does lead to some excesses.   The pet
squirrel's climbing up the slumped-over Uncle Billy, Harry's
receiving the Congressional Medal of Honor for saving the
lives of a transport-ful of soldiers, and the movie's con-
veniently ending on Christmas are unnecessary extras.   But
they don't obscure the script's basic strengths.

The concluding sequence begins with small, throwaway moments so fine that you wonder why Capra didn't give
his happy ending over to them entirely.   The first sign that
George is alive again is his bleeding lip, and he thinks it's
great to be alive and bleeding.   He cheers his ramshackle
car, with the door that alternately won't open and close.   He
wishes even Mr. Potter a "merry Christmas."   The irony
vanishes, momentarily, uncomfortably, when he passes a
Bedford Falls theatre playing The BELLS OF ST. MARY'S.
It reassuringly reappears when he delightedly greets the bank
examiner and the sheriff, who has a warrant for his arrest.
For the last ironic touch, he kisses the bannister knob that's

always coming loose in his hand.

What follows is hardly ironic, but it's affecting all the
same.   Perhaps the movie should have ended sooner, as
LOST HORIZON should have (much sooner), with his first,
slightly nutty, ecstatic embrace of life, leaving the rest implied.   Or maybe it should have left him enjoying Christmas
in a dingy little jail cell, with his family just visiting.   But
the main point to make is that the happy ending isn't con-
cocted.   The preceding nightmare sequence authenticates it.
After it, Capra could do practically anything he wanted.
And if he wanted to make the happy ending to end happy endings, he just about did.

James Stewart's George Bailey is, I think, one of the
handful of genuinely great characterizations in American movies, as powerful and original as Brando's Terry Malloy in
ON THE WATERFRONT, James Dean's Jim Stark in REBEL
WITHOUT A CAUSE, Katharine Hepburn's Alice Adams, or
her Mary Tyrone in LONG DAY'S JOURNEY INTO NIGHT.
His George Bailey has the controlled, modulated fire of his
Mr. Smith, but his impassioned speechmaking isn't the highlight this time.   His quieter, less showy scenes are more
challenging and complex--they don't fall into familiar dramatic patterns, as do the big speeches.   Stewart's range in
this one movie seems greater than his range over all his
previous movies.   Here you can see a new James Stewart
developing, a Stewart that the actor drew upon for later
roles.   (Disconnected fragments of him turn up in BROKEN
ARROW, The STRATTON STORY, THUNDER BAY,[23] etc.)

Here he doesn't seem constricted by a script, as he
does in unnatural, rigidly-conceived roles in films like
VERTIGO or The FAR COUNTRY, in which he's straining
to be something he isn't, rather than developing what he is.
Capra gives him room to stretch, to build his role, somewhat as John Ford let Henry Fonda's considered movements
and lanky body dictate pace and composition in YOUNG MR.
LINCOLN and MY DARLING CLEMENTINE.   Examples: As
George rushes upstairs to his children at the end of the movie, his legs buckle, his nervous exhaustion vivifying the
fact that he's so glad to be alive he can't stop even when
his body fails him.   --Conned into going to Mary's, he
saunters disdainfully up the walk to her, taking his time,
as she waits at the door (and the camera waits with her).
--Opposite Potter (and the camera) in Potter's office, George
tries to assert himself by sitting up straight in the low-bot-

tomed chair.   Stewart and Capra describe George visually:
George almost doesn't have to say a thing--it's all there to
see.   Without Stewart, with probably any other actor in the
lead role, Capra would have ended up with something less
fine.

In the scene in which George destroys the model
bridges and buildings and breaks down before his wife and
children, Stewart is light years away from his awkward, obviously unfelt outbursts in AFTER THE THIN MAN (1936)
and from Mr. Smith's crazy belligerence.   His bearing and
deadened voice are authoritative--you wouldn't be surprised
at anything George Bailey did at that point.   Stewart's lighter scenes with Donna Reed and Gloria Grahame are exquisite
and are reminiscent of some of his scenes with Margaret
Sullavan in SHOP AROUND THE CORNER and The MORTAL
STORM.   But in later scenes in the movie he's venturing
into territory that's new to him, as perhaps it would have
been to any American actor at the time.   (Even ALICE
ADAMS and The MAGNIFICENT AMBERSONS, which made
the family quarrel the bitter center of their portraits of
American families, did not have a father who, temporarily
at least, thought that his family would be better off without
him.)   Stewart's stricken features when he clutches his son
to himself make irrelevant the question of how good a life
George Bailey has led: life goes on around him, but he
can't take part in it.

Donna Reed's serenity and presence of mind as Mary
is an anchoring image for the movie.   She makes her presence felt with minimum flourish.   The casting of Jean Gale
as the girl Mary and Miss Reed as Mary the woman was inspired: both actresses have the same sort of "self-pos-
sessed dignity and intelligence," to use Manny Farber's description of Miss Reed.   They're such a perfect match that
they produce the illusion of reality.   There's no perceptible
gap in spirit between the girl Mary and the woman.   Miss
Gale's proprietary air, as of one possessing arcane knowledge, is superseded in Miss Reed's subtler air of composed
self-assurance.

The continuity of character between Bobbie Anderson
as the boy George and Stewart as the man is not quite as
smooth.   The congruencies seem more a matter of external
detail than of spirit, the visible signs of George's fervency
and wanderlust rather than the fervency and wanderlust themselves; at least they seem so as far as a performance can

be divided into internals and externals.

Lionel Barrymore is, I suppose, competent as Potter. He fills the role, but he doesn't expand it or give his villain the sinister dimensions Edward Arnold gave his Capra villains. The way he plays it, the role of evil incarnate is more a given than an active force, and it shouldn't be. The movie depends almost entirely on George's continuing response to the threat of Potter for any real, living sense of evil, thanks to Barrymore's complacency. There's no cutting edge to his voice on lines like, "He was a man of high ideals ... so-called, " just a slight emphasis to indicate that he knew there was supposed to be one. The character as written is static and as played it's still static. Capra's oversimplification of the role, his falling back on the dramatic convention of the out-and-out villain, wouldn't matter so much if Barrymore were sinister or funny or aggressively evil or in some way distinctive--his reminding one of Scrooge is not really distinction enough.

Thomas Mitchell as Uncle Billy fails to disguise an uncertainly-written part. He's given the more plot-heavy scenes--you can hear the whir of the mechanism--and some especially flat dialogue in the scene with Barrymore in the bank. He has two or three extenuating bits of comic business, but Capra's treatment of Billy's befuddlement is generally condescending and sentimental.

For the size of their roles, Samuel S. Hinds, as George's father, and Gloria Grahame, as Vi, make perhaps the strongest impressions of any of the actors in the movie. Hinds' contained, deliberate movements, suggesting a firm but considerate man, fix him in the memory, and his stationary presence in the dining room with George is, with the aid of a little imagination, the objective correlative of the stability of his life and of his place in his son's life. He seems made up of sheer endurance rather than, like George, intermittent inspiration.

Gloria Grahame's bittersweet peripheral performance is generally sliced in half in prints of the movie. Her Vi is as much an idealization of the "bad girl" as Mary is of the "good girl, " but the movie, I think, eliminates the traces of condescension to her that were in the final script. Capra dexterously tells her story in pockets of the movie: in the dance-floor scene, Vi's mock-surprise at turning around to see George, and his unintentional slighting of her when he

IT'S A WONDERFUL LIFE - James Stewart and Gloria Grahame

sees Mary, counterpoint George and Mary's reunion.

The wittiest performance is by Frank Hagney as Potter's bodyguard. His intentional inexpressiveness, his in-
conspicuousness, is (if you start to watch him closely) almost maddening, and George's late, abrupt acknowledgment
of his presence almost qualifies as comic catharsis.

There are a few scenes, some shots, and several
lines in IT'S A WONDERFUL LIFE that I don't like. I'm
unnaturally sensitive to its defects when I watch it. They
mar for me even the most powerful and beautiful passages.
I wince at the reaction shot of Janie crying after George's
explosion. I wish Mary wouldn't mechanically cry George's
name three times at the end of the telephone scene. I'm
suspicious of the troubles-are-all-over-they-lived-happily-
ever-after implications of the ending. And of a vague be-
happy-with-what-you've-got implication. I'm fearful of some
critic's possible, perverse interpretation of Mary as existing solely for George rather than (as I interpret her) for
herself and George.

But for all its faults and possible mis-readings, I
think it's one of the greatest American movies, as great as
Welles' The MAGNIFICENT AMBERSONS, Keaton's ONE
WEEK and The GENERAL, Sternberg's SCARLET EMPRESS,
Chaplin's The CIRCUS, the Marx Brothers' Paramounts, and
W. C. Fields' IT'S A GIFT, which are the best American
films I've seen. Among its innumerable, un-analyzable virtues I number the way George mutters, "... a walk, that's
all," after Mary, at a second-floor window of her home,
disappears inside. And Mary almost unable to say, "He
says it's the chance of a lifetime," to George as they stand
together at the phone. And a fantastic, twofold hat trick
with Ernie and George. And Harry's toast--"To my big
brother George--the richest man in town"--in the last scene.
And George's voice finally dominant in the communal singing
of "Auld Lang Syne" that ends the movie.

> It may not be too much of an exaggeration to say
> that [IT'S A WONDERFUL LIFE] is the most bril-
> liantly made motion picture of the 1940s so as-
> sured, so dazzling is its use of screen narrative
> to tell a fundamentally silly and banal story about
> the character of a small town.--Charles Higham,
> The Art of the American Film 1900-1971, 1973,

p. 195.

You can believe as much or as little of its story
as you like, but I defy you not to be moved by
IT'S A WONDERFUL LIFE ... through Capra's
brilliant direction of a well-written script, through
James Stewart's extraordinarily fine performance
(particularly in the later scenes as the desperate
man) ... IT'S A WONDERFUL LIFE has been
fashioned into an outstanding example of Ameri-
cana.... --Philip T. Hartung, Commonweal, Janu-
ary 3, 1947, p. 305.

Much too often this movie appeals to the heart at
the expense of the mind ... at still other times
the heart is simply used, on the mind, as a
truncheon. The movie does all this so proficient-
ly, and with so much genuine warmth, that I wasn't
able to get reasonably straight about it for quite a
while. --James Agee, The Nation, February 15,
1947, p. 193.

Notes

1. Bedford Falls, New York, in the final script (March 18,
   1946).

2. In the final script, heaven is a sunny, unfenced place,
   and Benjamin Franklin is one of the angels. The
   flashbacks are viewed over a glass-top-table screen.
   In the movie the angels are simply represented by
   blobs of light.

3. In the final script, Potter grumpily watches the boys
   from his house, and Mary Hatch watches from a
   bridge. George hits her in the face with a snowball,
   she cries, and he laughs at her. She stays, however, to watch admiringly as he rescues his brother.

4. In the final script, George's visit strengthens his father's
   resolve. Joseph, one of the angels, comments,
   "George never knew it, but he saved his father's
   business that day."

5. In the script, kids in Gower's drugstore take up George's
   "Nope, nope, nope" as he thanks Gower for a gift of

a suitcase.

6. A brief post-wedding scene is cut from most prints.

7. In a brief scene in the final script version, Clarence
    tells Joseph that he too wanted to get away, "to study
    music," but that his wife wanted him to work in her
    father's clock shop. So he put his music "into" the
    clocks: "You know, the chimes.... Today all over
    the world my chimes are ringing." And, in a scene
    cut from some prints, George helps the Martini
    family move from their hovel in Pottersfield to a
    new home in Bailey Park, and Sam and his wife
    drive by in a fancy new car and say hello.

8. Clarence says "nine," but the legend on the tombstone
    ("1911-1919") suggests that Harry was eight at the
    most.

9. "American Madness" (a good discussion of Capra's
    themes), Twenty-Four Times a Second (New York,
    Evanston and London, 1971), p. 131.

10. As the fantasy sequence begins, Clarence tells George
    that he has "no worries, no obligations, no $8,000
    to get." Then he goes on to show him the other
    side of his freedom: no friends, no family, no sense
    of identity.

11. WONDERFUL LIFE is one of two superb films I've seen
    that deal with frustrated wanderlust. The Pagnol-
    Alexander Korda MARIUS in the other.

12. The physical intensity of the scene is counterpointed by
    Sam Wainwright's cheerfully casual, mocking voice
    ("... still married to that old, broken-down building
    and loan...") as George and Mary listen to him on
    the same extension. It's also counterpointed by the
    comedy with Mary's nosy mother, which seems ir-
    relevant and even intrusive, and is solely intended to
    balance the drama. By contrast, the distancing com-
    edy with the Bailey boys and the maid, Annie, is al-
    so a deepening comedy, adding to the atmosphere of
    warmth and harmony in the Bailey home.

13. Pechter, op. cit., p. 128.

14. It's hard to see what Capra saw in the story except the
     basic idea--the hero's "I wish I'd never been born"
     --it's so flavorless and blandly didactic. The mov-
     ie's total re-structuring of the story--which consists
     only of the fantasy sequence, a short prologue, and
     a short epilogue--adds several emotional dimensions
     to it. For instance, in Stern's version, in the fan-
     tasy passages, George's father informs George that
     his only son Harry is dead, and George promptly re-
     calls the day that he was there to save Harry from
     drowning. The movie avoids such necessarily clum-
     sy a posteriori explaining by telling the story of
     George's life before beginning the fantasy sequence.
     Its revelation to George of his brother's early death
     is not just another point drily made.

15. The garish neon-and-noise, background horror-effects
     help too. The harsh spotlights and ghostly, illumi-
     nated, wind-whipped snow of the cemetery, the sha-
     dows the taxi spotlight casts through the decayed
     mansion, Mary's cries, and the violent reports of
     the shots Bert the cop takes at the fleeing George
     are right out of a nightmare.

16. The Nation, February 15, 1947, p. 193.

17. The Christian Science Monitor, May 5, 1961; interview
     by John C. Waugh.

18. I Lost It at the Movies (Boston-Toronto, 1965), p. 244.

19. Dimitri Tiomkin's instant-pathos music, which introduces
     Mary here, doesn't help either, though it's the lone
     false note of an otherwise unobtrusively effective
     score. It's there when and only when it's needed.
     In particular, Tiomkin's horror music partly catches,
     partly creates, the mood of the fantasy scenes.

20. Pechter, op. cit., p. 129.

21. Ibid., p. 132.

22. In his early film, ILLICIT INTERLUDE (1950), Ingmar
     Bergman attempts a similar reconciliation of despair
     and affirmation. But even John Simon admits that
     the "resigned or optimistic" ending is weak. And,
     actually, the earlier sudden-death, hooting-owl images

of despair are pretty pallid too.

23. George's crazy cackle when he touches his bleeding lip
     turns up here when the hero strikes oil.

PART II

ADAPTATIONS EAST AND WEST

Chapter 5

THE BITTER TEA OF GENERAL YEN

Columbia. 1932 (released 1933). 88 minutes.

Director: Frank Capra. Screenplay: Edward Paramore. Based on the novel by Grace Zaring Stone. Photography: Joseph Walker. Music: W. Frank Harling. Art Director: Stephen Goosson? Editor: Edward Curtis. Producer: Walter Wanger. Assistant Director: Buddy Coleman.

Cast: Barbara Stanwyck (Megan Davis), Nils Asther (General Yen), Gavin Gordon (Dr. Robert Strike), Toshia Mori (Mah-Li), Walter Connolly (Jones), Richard Loo (Captain Li), Lucien Littlefield (Mr. Jackson), Clara Blandick (Mrs. Jackson), Willie Fung, Ray Young (engineer), Emmett Corrigan (Bishop Harkness), Moy Ming (Dr. Lin), Robert Wayne (Rev. Bostwick), Knute Erickson (Dr. Hansen), Ella Hall (Mrs. Hansen), Arthur Millette (Mr. Pettis), Helen Jerome Eddy (Miss Reed), Martha Mattox (Miss Avery), Jessie Arnold (Mrs. Blake); Lillianne Leighton, Harriet Lorraine, Nora Cecil, Robert Bolder (missionaries), Miller Newman (Dr. Mott), Arthur Johnson (Dr. Shuler), Jessie Perry, Adda Gleason (Mrs. Bowman), Daisy Robinson (Mrs. Warden), Doris Louellyn (Mrs. Meigs), Milton Lee.

New Englander Megan Davis arrives in Shanghai to marry Robert Strike, a missionary. On her way to him by rickshaw, she encounters a Chinese bandit-general, Yen, when his limousine runs down her rickshaw boy. At the mission she finds missionaries gathered for the wedding ceremony, but Bob is not among them. When he does arrive, he enlists Megan's aid in an effort to save children trapped by warring factions in St. Andrew's Orphanage in Chapei. He forces General Yen to give him a safe conduct pass. Bob and Megan become separated, and she is virtually kidnapped by Yen. He holds her at his summer palace and

endeavors to break down the barriers that separate them.
He makes her quite comfortable, but she refuses to yield to
the handsome Yen. She is baffled by his nature, which embraces both an artistic sense and the use of violence. Jones,
Yen's financial adviser, informs him that his (Yen's) mistress, Mah-Li, and his aide, Captain Li, are betraying him
to the enemy. Yen orders the death of the two as punishment. Megan intercedes for the girl, promising to answer
for her conduct. Mah-Li betrays Yen again and flees the
palace. Yen, however, cannot bring himself to kill Megan,
and she tries to overcome her resistance to him. She unwittingly interrupts him as he is about to sip a cup of poisoned tea. She offers herself to him but can't help crying
in weakness, and Yen drinks the tea.

It's fairly simple and elementary, but as often as not
its simplicity works to the advantage of The BITTER TEA
OF GENERAL YEN. This untypical Capra film is alternately
artificial and exquisite, drab prose alternating with rich po-
etry. Its simplicity sometimes seems a lazy solution to
thorny esthetic problems--as with the characters of Megan
Davis and Jones and a long dinner-and-cards sequence which
dispenses with half the plot and one of the characters. At
other times the movie is more purposefully simple and blunt
--as with the character of General Yen and the climax, Yen's
death, a reaffirmation of the movie's and the characters'
basic simplicity.

Nils Asther and Barbara Stanwyck may co-star in The
BITTER TEA OF GENERAL YEN (hers is actually the name
above the title), but it's General Yen's movie, for several
reasons. First, Megan is not really an equal but a player
in Yen's drama, [1] though she isn't the mere prop that the
other characters are. And, although the character of Megan
is supposed to be repressed, cold, limited in its very conception, Megan's woodenness is often hard to distinguish
from the woodenness of Miss Stanwyck, who has trouble
modulating her voice. Her uncertain performance even more
decidedly subordinates Megan to Yen in importance. Finally,
to say that Nils Asther gives the only interesting performance
in the movie is not really giving him his due. His General
makes the movie, which could have been an empty exercise
in romantic effects and a bland lesson on the intransigence
of human nature.

Asther's Yen is both witty and human. Asther deftly
plays off against each other Yen's distancing Oriental wit

and pride and his genuine desire to comprehend Megan's
Christian philosophy. In the space of minutes, Yen can appear amused, tender, solicitous, menacing, wise, and las-
civious, in that or any order, and Asther blends this solicitude, menace, amusement, tenderness, and lasciviousness
without marking transitions. These various incarnations
seem facets of Yen's attitude toward life, not successive
poses, but a continuing revelation of character. It's a role
that could have passed on style alone, but Asther gives General Yen, and the movie, substance as well.

        Pauline Kael, in an early essay on movies, noted:
"There are people who can sit around for hours discussing
early films, giving detailed accounts of dialogue, action,
gesture, even costume, exchanging remembered reactions to
Colin Clive, or what Nils Asther was like in The BITTER
TEA OF GENERAL YEN...."[2] What people probably remember about Asther's General are the witty details, such
as his suggestively shaking Strike's lapel as he asks him if
he has "ever heard singsong girls." Or his placing his cig-
arette, without turning his head or breaking stride, in a
guard's mouth as he sweeps by him into Megan's room. Or
his glance heavenward as he comments on Strike's taste in
women: "He seems to have excellent taste--in some things."
Or his putting Jones in his place by straightening the latter's
tie, tapping his chest, pulling his dusty hat down over his
eyes and hitting it, then smartly wiping the dust off his hands
as he walks away.

        In a sometimes coarsely-written film, Yen stands out
as one of the most skillfully-drawn, fully-realized characters
in any Capra film.

        His callousness and Megan's Christian charity are
both introduced in broad, unmistakable terms. But his dry,
matter-of-fact "Yes" to Megan's "You've run down my rickshaw boy" is an intentional surprise, while the surprise of
her offer of a kerchief for his cut forehead, just after she
has exclaimed, "How can you be so unfeeling?", is only partly intentional. Is her forgetfulness of the accident victim
here being underscored? Or, more probably, is this just
supposed to be an example of her charity towards all? Her
sudden solicitude is an artificial way of comparing, or con-
trasting, the two, and the shift of gears in Megan to make
a point (either one) is so violent it's comical. (The scene
is also a weak introduction of the movie's main motif of the
handkerchief.)

Yen's fascinating, elusive character is economically
established by this scene, and you can see the attraction he
has for her: "But I can't understand it--the owner of the
car looked so civilized," she says later. And, despite the
artifice, you can even see how her, perhaps mechanical, act
of unexpected kindness would intrigue him.

Megan's rigid nature is contrasted with Yen's relative
openness and flexibility. Her rigidness ("finest old Puritan
family in New England") is essential--for Yen's personal
drama. It annoys and torments him, distracting his attention from a raging civil war. He tests it to find out if
there's something to it and discovers that it is not, to his
regret, a hypocritical guise, but something deeper. Or (Miss
Stanwyck's performance creates some accidental ambiguity)
perhaps it's Yen's very experimentation that strengthens Megan's Christian resolve, deepening it so that it finally ceases
to seem, as it does at first (unintentionally?), shallow.
Even near the end, when there should be no question of Megan's sincerity, Miss Stanwyck's hollow delivery of lines almost renders Megan's true Puritanism suspect.

If The BITTER TEA had been a "Nils Asther" rather
than a "Barbara Stanwyck" movie, the story could have been
told strictly from Yen's point-of-view, as it should have
been. Megan is a more or less static character--that's the
point, of course. She exists dramatically, in fact if not intent, solely as an adjunct to General Yen. Her disillusionment at the hands of Mah-Li is inevitable, and the script
dwells on it needlessly. Miss Stanwyck, Capra, and Edward
Paramore accidentally subordinate Megan to Yen, when they
should have done it intentionally. They leave her stranded
in scenes with Yen and Mah-Li in which she monotonously
repeats her Christian trust in others in lines like, "I'm
proud of you, Mah-Li. I knew you were a good girl," and,
"I'm quite sure she's good." Megan, like Mr. Deeds and
Mr. Smith, is so bland and uncorrupt that she seems to
come from another planet. But her purity of soul is never
meant to be taken comically, and it's difficult to take it any
other way, it's so stiffly expressed. Neither actress nor
director seems to know how to develop her simplicity or
make it vital; they just, unproductively, keep returning to it.
Only Yen's obsession with it and with her lends it a little
dramatic authority.

Yen uses every means at his disposal, except force,
to draw her to him. Though he can, as he tells her, "com-

pel" the loyalty of others, he in no way tries to compel Megan's love. He explains the humaneness of his execution of
prisoners of war: there is no rice for them, and isn't it
better to be shot than to starve to death?   He alters his appearance in an effort to make himself appealing to her.
Though Megan gives him no way of knowing it, he is, from
the first, appealing to her. A dream of Megan's enchanting-
ly explains the nature of his appeal. That dream (and its
context) is one of the movie's two memorable sequences--the
ending is the other--and is worth recounting in full.

It's evening. The scene outside Megan's window,
earlier in the day the scene of executions, is now an exotic
land of fantasy. Thus, scenes of the Orient at its most violent and its most alluring occur just beyond her window.
The camera, waiting outside, catches her just as she steps
out. It's as if she were stepping into Paradise. The music,
like the change to color in The WIZARD OF OZ, signals the
entry into a dreamland. Sounds of flutes and lute-like in-
struments mingle with subdued shouts and cries from soldiers
across the brook from Megan's balcony, which, like a royal
box, affords her an ideal view of the scene. An obviously
artificial moon, which Yen says his people call the "spring
moon" or the "cherry blossom moon," is perched over a
pagoda in the background. A truck arrives with girls, whom
the soldiers eagerly help down. They all scatter. Drooping
willows and the brook frame a soldier and his girl on a
bench. A shot of the spring moon dissolves into a shot of
Megan's forehead, as if the sensuous spirit of the scene were
entering her.

The music changes--once lulling, it's now disorienting,
out of sync with the action. In this dream within a dream,
a savage, lustful Oriental in sinister black (Yen, in witty
caricature) smashes in Megan's door and approaches her.
His "claws" frame her. As he caresses her, another phantom (masked, with a white hat) leaps in through the window
and quickly disposes of the monster. She removes his mask
--Yen again. Yen the romantic; Yen the villainous. Even in
this brief escape from reality, from herself, they both appear, but here she can separate the two. The heroic Yen
embraces her. They kiss, as they never do outside her
dream; the backdrop swirls dizzyingly behind a close-up of
Megan. The music halts abruptly as Megan wakes up. She
is frightened by the implications of her dream, in which she
succumbs, subconsciously, to the spell of Yen and the Orient.
(Later, when she first tries on a shimmering, spangled dress

that recalls her dream kiss, she catches herself, as she
does here, and changes it.) Yen comes out onto the balcony
from her room and tries to engage her in conversation.
Megan rebuffs him.

The music, which stopped with the end of her dream,
starts up again when Yen leaves, its cessation underlining
Megan's conscious effort to resist him, the resumption suggesting that the seductiveness of the atmosphere is less
threatening to her than that of Yen.   The character of Megan
comes fully to life only in this sequence, in part because she
says very little.   In other scenes, Capra and Miss Stanwyck
seem to have no idea of how she would talk or what she
would say.

The ending is brutally fatalistic, yet Yen's ritualistic
suicide is one of the most romantic scenes in movies.   When
they first meet, when Megan tells him that her rickshaw boy
may be dying, he replies, "If so, he's very fortunate.   Life
even at its best is hardly endurable."   His later placing of
his power and wealth in Megan's hands is an expression not
of any faith he has in others (including Megan and Mah-Li),
but simply of his love for Megan.   He knows Mah-Li will
betray him.   His cynicism is again borne out by this climactic scene, by Megan's inability to respond to him, even
though she wants to and tries to.   Her own faith is shattered, but her nature remains.   She wants to surrender to
him physically, but must force herself to.   She imitates
Mah-Li, giving him a pillow; Yen's hands frame her face
for a few seconds, and her dream seems to be coming true.
But she can't help crying, and he removes his hands.   The
delicacy and restraint of his movements; the visual tact and
understatement; the music and the absence of words; all
make the scene most affecting.

Yen recognizes Megan's transformation for what it is
--a superficial, willed change, a matter of a spangled dress.
He reluctantly rejects her hollow acquiescence, his suicide
reaffirming that part of him which is inflexible, as Megan's
tears reaffirm that part of her which is inflexible.   His suicide reaffirms his words to her: "Do you think that General
Yen could accept anything that the heart did not freely give?"
Yen's suicide, his rejection of her sacrifice of herself, is
his final act of love for her, a greater demonstration of it
than his sacrifice of power.

Jones, an otherwise expendable character (well-acted

by Walter Connolly), provides, as he and Megan sail back to
Shanghai, the epilogue--just words, but in the context of
what has preceded it, as powerful as images: "Yen was
crazy. He said we never really die. We only change. He
was nuts about cherry trees. Maybe he's a cherry tree now.
Maybe he's the wind that's pushing that sail. Maybe he's
the wind that's playing around your hair. Oh, it's all a lot
of hooey. I'm drunk. Just the same, I hope when I cool
off the guy that changes me sends me where Yen is. And
I bet I'll find you there too."

Jones' rambling softens the harshness of the ending,
but I don't think his admission of tipsiness is intended as a
disclaimer. There's the ring of the eternal in the inflexi-
bility of the characters of Yen and Megan. And Jones' images of reincarnation recall the Megan of her dream, the
Megan free of earthly restraints. His words also recall
Yen's admission to Megan that he planned to kill her after
Mah-Li's betrayal: "I was coming to your room to kill you
and then follow you to some celestial garden where there's
no General Yen and no Megan Davis, just you and I." In
other words, what earth cannot resolve, heaven can, the differences that, maddeningly, sometimes separate human beings.

Stone, Grace Zaring.   The Bitter Tea of General Yen.
        Indianapolis: The Bobbs-Merrill Company, 1930, 322
        pages.

In making the movie The BITTER TEA OF GENERAL
YEN, Edward Paramore and Frank Capra did not so much
adapt the Grace Zaring Stone novel as rewrite it. This is
not to say that it's a bad or mediocre book that they bought
for the title and then junked. It's good in its own right,
thin, but more even than the movie. It's never as bad as
the movie at its worst, never as good as the movie at its
best. Why Paramore and Capra would take a perfectly decent
novel, ignore its strengths, and fashion almost incidental material into a perfectly decent movie which hardly even resembles the book, I don't know, unless they assumed that the
movie-going public was not ready for a pointed examination
of the motivations of the Christian missionary, but was ready
for miscegenation. What's so baffling about the two works
is that each in its own way is good yet bears so little resemblance to the other that it might have been composed independently.

To begin with, Bob, Megan's fiancé, and Dr. Strike
are two different characters in the book. Bob, in fact, never
appears in its present, and Dr. Strike is a major character,
a missionary whom Megan admires. The movie all but dis-
cards him and the book's other missionaries and drastically
alters the role of Megan. The book is told from Megan's
point-of-view; it's her story, not Yen's, which might seem
to justify the size of Miss Stanwyck's part in the movie,
and which would if she were playing Megan of the book.
But she isn't, and the differences between the two Megans
shed some light on the puzzling hollowness of the movie's
Megan.

The book's scope is wider. It picks Megan up first
as a child. It provides a context for Megan's missionary
spirit; the movie takes her religious zeal, and Bob Strike's,
for granted. In the movie, Megan and Bob may be ineffec-
tual, even inept, but they're sincere, and nothing but sincere.
The role of missionary is just one of several that the book's
Megan might have adopted. When she was seventeen she devoted herself to an unrequited love for Bob: "... Megan fell
in love with Bob, that is to say, she decided to focus on him
all the ardors and enthusiasms ... of which she was capa-
ble." When Bob, a medical missionary, asks her to marry
him and go with him to China, Megan adopts his religious
enthusiasm: "Up to now she had treated her religious beliefs with some indifference, sometimes with scorn, but Bob's
orthodoxy, his desire to serve, seemed to her now to have
the only beauty and dignity."

The book's basic strength lies in its characterization
of Megan as rejecting the easy options in life and the blatant
hypocrisy of those around her and yet not knowing what she
should make of herself. General Yen, near the end, con-
fronts Megan with her real self: "... this love you talk
about ... seems to me only an outlet for your irresistible
energy. It is energy. I have not seen in you any real concern over living harmoniously with your fellow men." She
is herself, unknowingly, innocently, hypocritical.

The book suffers from a certain bloodlessness and
aridity, but all the characters fit in and make sense. In the
movie only Yen makes dramatic sense at all times. Mrs.
Jackson, Miss Reed, Bob Strike, Mah-Li, and often even
Megan are just cogs in the plot. In the book, Mrs.
Jackson, a missionary, spends her time ignoring the Chinese

rather than ministering to them; the movie reduces her hypocrisy to one line about the "immoral" Chinese. In the
book, Miss Reed, another mission worker, who sees herself
as an heroic martyr, endangers the lives of others through
her unnecessary martyrdom. In the movie she's only a turn
in the plot. The Bob Strike of the movie assumes the role
of the book's Dr. Strike in the action but little of his meaning for Megan as the only missionary who truly attempts to
understand and interact with the Chinese. It's the movie's
jettisoning, in effect, of these characters that accounts for
the emptiness of the opening portions of the movie, which are
distinguished only be the first appearance of Yen and by some
finely detailed battle scenes.

In the movie, Megan's Christian charity is supposed
to be taken at face value. She is made to appear a fool for
trusting Mah-Li, but she's a sincere fool, and there is never
a hint that she has any but the highest motives for everything
she does. In the book, Megan unconsciously uses the other
characters--primarily Mah-Li and Yen--as tools with which
to express herself religiously. In the movie she rather dolt-
ishly insists on Mah-Li's goodness and seems genuinely interested in her welfare. The Mah-Li of the book is just a
"cause" for Megan--women's rights. She doesn't just vaguely want to help Mah-Li--she wants to free her from her con-
cubinage.

The movie tries to have it both ways, to have a hero
and a heroine, by fleshing out the role of Yen, a secondary
character in the book, and by retaining, superficially, the
importance of Megan. It doesn't have it both ways, but it
does, surprisingly, compensate for its shell of a Megan with
its General Yen and its two fine sequences, neither of which
is more than hinted at in the book. (The moon-dream sequence incorporates a few scattered lines and incidents from
the book; Yen's suicide is original in its entirety.) The movie, ingeniously, transforms the relationship between Megan
and Yen from a primarily impersonal, socio-cultural one into
a personal, romantic one. Love, rather than a flaw in the
age-old Chinese order, brings about Yen's downfall. Early
in the movie, Megan's dream presents Yen as a romantic
hero for her, and Yen is strongly attracted to her. In the
novel, Megan is, by contrast, slightly repelled by the smoothness of Yen's skin, and Yen, at the end, refuses Megan's
plea to let Mah-Li live. Only by chance does she live. Megan at first isn't even sorry that Mah-Li is probably dead;

she just feels betrayed by the General.   The General Yen of
the film puts his love for Megan above military strategy.

In Ms. Stone's book, Christianity is just another religion, like Buddhism, which leaves China's routines and rigid
social order unaffected.   Only once does Yen allow a hu-
manistic, Western spirit to affect him, when Shultz (the
Jones of the movie) invites him to escape with Megan and
him even though Yen's presence will endanger their lives.
In the Capra-Paramore version, Yen allows his love for this
eccentric foreigner to destroy him and his sense of order.
The book ends on a subdued note of futility, on Megan's and
Dr. Strike's puzzlement at their inability to "save" General
Yen, to save China.   The movie closes on a sustained, sub-
lime romantic note.

> One of the most interesting and least cloying of
> Frank Capra's films.....--Pauline Kael, The New
> Yorker.

> ... the general spikes his drink with a heart-
> stopper and flits out with the girl stroking his
> hand.--Variety, November 18, 1932.

> Unfortunately for the picture the war stuff is lim-
> ited....   After the Chinese general goes on the
> make for the white girl the picture goes blah.--
> Variety, January 17, 1933.

> ... BITTER TEA will remain forever as one of
> my pet pictures.--Frank Capra, The Name above
> the Title, 1971, p. 142.

> Just for the sake of the record, the number-one
> story about China was done as a picture and some
> years ago and in Hollywood at that, almost without
> modern plumbing and without benefit of the Signifi-
> cant Word, by Frank Capra, whose picture was
> called The BITTER TEA OF GENERAL YEN.--Otis
> Ferguson, The Film Criticism of Otis Ferguson,
> 1971, p. 152.

Notes

1.   This may be partly unintentional: female characters in

even Capra's best movies tend to be less certainly
developed than male, as if Capra did not know what
to do with them and his writers couldn't tell him.
Claudette Colbert in IT HAPPENED ONE NIGHT and
Donna Reed in IT'S A WONDERFUL LIFE are two
decided exceptions to this general rule.

2.   Pauline Kael, "Movies, the Desperate Art," Film: An
     Anthology, ed. Daniel Talbot (Berkeley and Los Ange-
     les, 1967), p. 69.

Chapter 6

LOST HORIZON

Hilton, James. <u>Lost Horizon</u>. New York: William Morrow, 1933, 277 pages.

The prologue is tantalizing, and the epilogue concludes elliptically on four successive, imaginative notes. Unfortunately, the story itself leaves nothing to the imagination. Movies are sometimes accused of being too literal, of being inimical to fantasy because whatever the camera records becomes fact, "real." But books can "show" too much too. The fantasy kingdom of Shangri-La in <u>Lost Horizon</u> is all too palpable, and not surprisingly, the best parts of the book are those set furthest from Shangri-La, those that suggest rather than show.

Hilton's Utopia is static, inert, more an attitude or a philosophy than a subject for a story. Shangri-La is a combination rest home, commune, art gallery, and library, and all <u>Lost Horizon</u> amounts to is a tour and an explanation, within a dramatic frame. Sometimes, even when it's not that good, I can sense the basic attraction of a fantasy, but the attraction of <u>Lost Horizon</u> escapes me. It's rather like Stevenson's Dr. <u>Jekyll and Mr. Hyde</u> in its separation of man into good (Jekyll, meditation, moderation) and bad (Hyde, passion, violence). It over-simplifies the human condition. There's no struggle, just solution. The book's ideal of moderation is itself moderately mechanical, a cure-all.

The simplicity of the fantasy is matched by the simplistic characterizations. Conway is a good beginning for a character--essentially "lazy," "passionless," disillusioned, cynically detached, but stimulated to action by the prospect of danger--but he's not developed. He may seem to be, because Hilton offers a thumbnail description of him every chapter or so, but it's the same description in different words. Chang and the High Lama are simply mouthpieces

for philosophy and history, some dull, some interesting.
And the businessman Barnard and Captain Mallinson are the
worst kind of type characters: one-note, naggingly repeated.

LOST HORIZON. Columbia. 1937. Longest extant version:
118 minutes. (LOST HORIZON OF SHANGRI-LA - reissue
title).

Director, Producer: Frank Capra. Screenplay: Robert
Riskin. Based on the novel by James Hilton. Photography:
Joseph Walker. Aerial Photography: Elmer Dyer. Musical
Score: Dimitri Tiomkin. Art Director: Stephen Goosson.
Editors: Gene Havlick, Gene Milford. Musical Director:
Max Steiner. Special Effects: E. Roy Davidson, Ganahl
Carson. Set Decorations: Babs Johnstone. Costumes:
Ernst Dryden. Voices: Hall Johnson Choir. Technical Ad-
viser: Harrison Forman. Assistant Director: C. C. Cole-
man.

     Cast: Ronald Colman (Robert Conway), Jane Wyatt
(Sondra), John Howard (George Conway), Margo (Maria),
H. B. Warner (Chang), Sam Jaffe (High Lama), Edward
Everett Horton (Alexander P. Lovett), Thomas Mitchell (Hen-
ry Barnard), Isabel Jewell (Gloria Stone), Willie Fung and
Victor Wong (bandit leaders), Noble Johnson (leader of porters), Hugh Buckler (Lord Gainsford), John Miltern (Car-
stairs), Lawrence Grant, John Burton (Wynant), John T.
Murray (Meeker), Max Rabinowitz (Seiveking), Wyrley Birch
(missionary), John Tettener (Montaigne), Boyd Irwin, Sr.
(Assistant Foreign Secretary), Leonard Mudie (Foreign Secre-
tary), David Clyde (Steward), Neil Fitzgerald and Derby
Clark (radio operators), Val Durand (Talu), Ruth Robinson
and Margaret McWade (missionaries), Dennis D'Auburn (avi-
ator), Milton Owen (Fenner), Carl Stockdale (missionary);
Beatrice Curtis, Mary Lou Dix, Beatrice Blinn, Arthur Ran-
kin (passengers), George Chan (Chinese priest), Eric Wilton,
Richard Loo (Shanghai Airport official); Ernesto Zambrano,
Richard Master, Alex Shoulder, Manuel Kalili (servants);
Barry Winton, Robert Corey, Henry Mowbray, Wedgwood
Nowell (Englishmen); Chief Big Tree, Eli Casey, Richard
Robles, James Smith (porters).

     Caught up in the Japanese invasion of the Chinese
frontier city of Baskul, British Consul Robert Conway takes
charge of the evacuation by plane to Shanghai of some 90

white residents. Conway himself boards the last plane,
which also carries his younger brother George; Gloria, a
bitter young woman with tuberculosis; Barnard, an American
businessman on the run; and Lovett, a jittery paleontologist.
A stowaway, a mysterious Mongolian, kills the pilot, and
next morning the passengers find that the plane is headed in
the wrong direction. Holding them at bay with a pistol, the
new pilot attempts to fly the plane up 20,000 feet over the
Tibetan peaks. An engine failure sends the plane crashing
into a mountainside. The pilot dies, but a party of Tibetans
led by the English-speaking Chang rescues the five survivors.
He guides them through a blizzard to the gigantic lamasery
of Shangri-La in the temperate, fertile Valley of the Blue
Moon.

The visitors are received with great hospitality and
are housed in luxurious quarters, but they soon discover that
they are virtual prisoners. The High Lama of Shangri-La,
a French priest named Father Perrault, who came to the valley in 1713, sends for Conway and tells him that he has
found a secret for living which eliminates struggle and emphasizes beauty and peace. People in Shangri-La are happy
and live to a great age. Realizing that he was about to die,
the High Lama, impressed by Conway's philosophical works,
had him kidnapped and brought to him. He asks Conway to
take his place as High Lama. Conway, already in love with
a girl, Sondra, who has lived in the lamasery all her life,
agrees to stay. But Conway's brother plots to escape with
Maria, a woman who looks 20 but is actually 66. Chang
says that if she leaves, she'll turn into an old hag. Maria
denies Chang's story, and, his faith shaken, Conway agrees
to leave with her and his brother. The High Lama dies, and
the three flee into the mountains as his funeral procession
files up the valley walls to the temple. Later, Maria, exhausted, reverts to old age and dies. George, mad, jumps
to his death. Conway, suffering total amnesia, is picked up
by natives, carried to Shanghai, and is on his way back to
London when his memory returns. He escapes his guardians
and returns to the Valley of the Blue Moon.

For Frank Capra, Lost Horizon was a strikingly poor
choice of material. The book's slight qualities are static,
pictorial, quiet, and Capra's talent was to make things move.
Capra tries to make things move--with an avalanche, a plane
crash, a chase on horseback--but the book wins. The action
is dull, filler material, and the movie's better moments are
the quieter ones. The book provides no story, and the movie

goes about Shangri-La from scene to scene vainly looking
for one. The material clearly calls for a calm, unexcited
treatment, but Capra, Riskin, and Walker fight this tendency, throwing in bits of action and moving the camera more
than it needs to be moved.

It's a critical dictum (probably false) that it's easier
to turn a mediocre book into a good movie than it is to turn
a good book into a good movie. Someone like Satyajit Ray
might be able to make a good movie of Lost Horizon; someone who is at home in quieter surroundings and with a more
leisurely tempo. In his enchanting KANCHENJUNGHA, Ray
finds time for establishing his characters, for establishing
the atmosphere of their mountainside retreat, and for show-
ing how that setting works on them. For all that was spent
on sets, props, and effects, LOST HORIZON has a surprisingly weak sense of place, due in part to the hopping-about
effect. With all the film's luxuriance in sets and scenery,
Capra takes no time to luxuriate. He must be on his way.
For example, there's a scene with Jane Wyatt, a deer, and
a waterfall. But it's too brief and it's wrecked by Dimitri
Tiomkin's push-button beauties-of-nature music. (Tiomkin
takes the action interludes and wrings them for all they're
worth.) Capra is caught between his static material and his
inclination to spur the story on, and he loses both ways: no
story, no atmosphere.

Most of the picture's romantic, pastoral conceptions
are trite. In what must surely have qualified for most embarrassing scene of 1937, a nude (implied) Jane Wyatt, taking her cue from Tarzan, listens as a squirrel, taking his
cue from Cheetah, warns her of Conway's approach. The
supposedly exotically gentle people of the valley are conventionally romanticized rustics. Sondra, who might also be
caught wishing out loud that the spirit of Christmas would
last all year, wishes that "the whole world could come to
the valley." The romantic scenes with Conway and Sondra
are conventional too, but they do afford one nice verbal conceit in which she's a plane and he's her shadow. Other
"exotic" elements are embarrassingly familiar from science-
fiction movies: the foreigner (Chang) who surprises the trav-
ellers with his perfect English, the pretty girls, the "deli-
cious" food. FIRE MAIDENS FROM OUTER SPACE is almost a remake.

Everything seems to go wrong with the High Lama's
scenes. One significant difference between his scenes and

the scenes with Chang is the scoring. Tiomkin feels compelled to add to the makeup and lighting effects for the High Lama, an act of misplaced homage, while the Conway-Chang exchanges are allowed to produce their own little magic, without music. Chang is thus less formidable, but less laughable, and the simplicity and lightness of his scenes with Conway, combined with H. B. Warner's unassuming manner and air of informal dignity, command more respect than the intensified High Lama scenes.

The first conversation between Conway and the High Lama is introduced with a rather dumb line ("The High Lama is waiting to see you"), and Riskin seems to be aware of starting-off-on-the-wrong-foot when he has Thomas Mitchell kid it ("Low Lama"). But dubious dialogue checked by comedy is still dubious.

Conway's identification of the High Lama with the founder of Shangri-La, Father Perrault, might best be done subtly, with perhaps a subjective shot, as Conway notices the giveaway solitary foot--one of Perrault's legs was amputated--and a quiet reaction shot. But there's a close shot of a crutch, a pan down to the High Lama's foot, over-reaction shots, and finally Conway's spoken acknowledgment of his discovery. All that's missing is a subtitle: "The High Lama = Father Perrault." Capra, with all his technical proficiency, is reduced to rank clumsiness.

But the worst thing about the High Lama scenes is the High Lama himself. Sam Jaffe, a more amusing gargoyle in Josef von Sternberg's great, glorious SCARLET EMPRESS, looks and acts like a cross between a mindless zombie and the Phantom of the Opera. He has a manic look more suited to Eduardo Ciannelli's religious fanatic in GUNGA DIN, and if there's anything his scenes don't need, it's a touch of fanaticism. They're already--in subject and treatment--slightly crazy.

Capra, who usually doesn't make mistakes with the camera, makes several in LOST HORIZON. He introduces Jane Wyatt, who doesn't figure in the story until some time later, with a "co-starring" close shot when Conway first sees her. It only lasts a second or two, but in effect, it stops the movie. And, to get some movement into the movie, Capra twice has the camera pointlessly travel with the characters. He makes the opposite error in an early Conway-Chang scene in which the camera remains static for too

long. Theoretically the height of unobtrusiveness, a long,
single-take scene with the camera stationary is actually the
most self-conscious of camera set-ups. Then there is an
example of ignorance of what Otis Ferguson called "the little
cares that have to be expended on static things if they are
to create a general forward movement":[1] a brief insert of
the careening passengers inside a plane as it skids to a halt.
The insert lasts just long enough to destroy the illusion of
movement.

In one area only is the movie at all successful: in the
character of Robert Conway. Hilton's good beginning for
Conway is carried further by Colman, whose performance
gives the movie a center. It's not a dominating performance,
but it does give the movie something to return to after this
bit of comedy or that bit of action has distracted it. One
certainly isn't dazzled by the unimaginative Shangri-La one
sees, but one is sympathetic to the reflection one sees of it
in Colman's eyes. Colman's Conway embodies some of the
qualities of life in Shangri-La: deliberativeness, disenchantment with the outside world, longing for peace.

Only in the character of Conway does the theme of
dreams fulfilled find adequate expression. Barnard, Lovett,
and Gloria, true, find their Utopias, but as though they were
apples waiting to be plucked from a tree. Conway's fulfill-
ment is less mechanical: though his brother George's one-
note grumbling is as annoying as his counterpart Mallinson's
in the novel, it makes itself felt in the doubts it breeds in
Robert, or, more precisely, in the uncertainty that shows
in Colman's face.

Shangri-La is about as flat an idea of a fantasy land
as there is. You're either there or you're not. It's only
when the possibility arises that Conway may have to leave
it, unwillingly, that it begins to mean something. Shangri-
La, physically all too believable (and dull), comes to life
only when Conway's spiritual doubts grow. When Maria's
story shakes Conway's belief, Shangri-La is once again just
a dream to him, as it is to everyone. Capra evidently
sensed that the scene in which Conway decides to leave was
just about the most important one in the movie: he shuts
off all potentially distracting sounds and movement and gives
Colman sole responsibility for carrying it. The sudden
break in rhythm is as riveting as an unannounced pause in
an Ozu movie.

A briefer, perhaps even more affecting scene is Conway's last, anguished look at the valley as he leaves it, as he thinks, forever. It's an example of the power of the moment in movies. The emotion evident in his face momentarily obliterates the trivialities of the preceding 90 minutes. You forget that what Conway is leaving is a Tinker Toy nirvana. The rest of the movie is still silly and trivial, but it has, entirely illogically, produced a memorable moment.

One review of LOST HORIZON had the movie ending with Conway heading "desperately again for Shangri-La."[2] Such an ending would have matched the book's (and been very similar in spirit to the brilliant summarizing conclusion of CHILDREN OF PARADISE), but, alas, the movie ends as Conway reaches Shangri-La: as reviewers complained at the time, the Capra happy ending, and no desperation.

Ross Hunter, with his unerring taste, chose to remake LOST HORIZON, the least of Capra's classics. Still, he could have improved on the first version of Hilton's book since it wasn't really Capra material to begin with. Its placidity, in fact, might at first seem to be suited to Charles Jarrott, who's a very dull director. But Capra films tend to be remade not only badly, but as musicals, and the songs in the LOST HORIZON remake are more intrusive than the action was in the original. Any hope for continuity is shot to hell in the middle of the film by six straight musical numbers, one for every character except (thank God!) the High Lama. The songs serve only to emphasize the sappiness of the original ideas. The movie is generally just dull; only the numbers are actually embarrassing. Sally Kellerman and Olivia Hussey prancing through a library is not quite what James Hilton had in mind.

The redeeming feature of the Capra version was Ronald Colman's performance. But Peter Finch's Conway, along with the continuity, is shredded by the songs--though it seems he anticipated such an eventuality and refrained from acting, and fortunately nothing is lost. The High Lama stuff isn't cuckoo at least; the reverence is soft-pedalled. But Charles Boyer's droning hardly seems mystically inspired. They could have used the book's ending this time. Instead they use the other movie's and go it one better: someone sings the title tune over it. Thanks, Ross.

Notes

1. The Film Criticism of Otis Ferguson (Philadelphia,
    1971), p. 75.

2. Scholastic, March 20, 1937, p. 22.

Chapter 7

YOU CAN'T TAKE IT WITH YOU

Columbia. 1938. 127 minutes.

Director, Producer: Frank Capra. Screenplay: Robert
Riskin. Based on the play by George S. Kaufman and Moss
Hart. Photography: Joseph Walker. Musical Score: Di-
mitri Tiomkin. Musical Director: Morris Stoloff. Art Di-
rector: Stephen Goosson. Associate: Lionel Banks. Edi-
tor: Gene Havlick. Costumes: Irene, Bernard Newman.
Assistant Director: Arthur S. Black. Sound: Edward
Bernds.

Cast: Edward Arnold (Anthony P. Kirby), Jean
Arthur (Alice Sycamore), Lionel Barrymore (Martin Vander-
hof), James Stewart (Tony Kirby), Spring Byington (Penny
Sycamore), Mischa Auer (Kolenkhov), Ann Miller (Essie
Carmichael), Dub Taylor (Ed Carmichael), Samuel S. Hinds
(Paul Sycamore), Donald Meek (Poppins), H. B. Warner
(Ramsey), Halliwell Hobbes (Mr. DePinna), Mary Forbes
(Mrs. Anthony Kirby), Eddie Anderson (Donald), Lillian Yar-
bo (Rheba), Charles Lane (Henderson), Harry Davenport
(judge), Irving Bacon (Henry), James Burke and Ward Bond
(detectives), Clarence Wilson (John Blakely), Josef Swickard
(professor), Ann Doran (Maggie O'Neill), Christian Rub
(Schmidt), Bodil Rosing (Mrs. Schmidt); Pierre Watkin, Edwin Maxwell, Russell Hicks (attorneys), Byron Foulger (Kirby's assistant), Ian Wolfe (Kirby's secretary), Chester Clute
(Hammond), James Flavin (jailer), Pert Kelton and Kit Guard
(inmates), Dick Curtis (strong-arm man), Edward Keane
(board member), Edward Hearn (court attendant); Robert
Greig, John Hamilton, Major Sam Harris (diners).

But since none of us has reached the ultimate
peace of Nirvana, the inner battle between brutality
and compassion agonizes the spiritually advanced,

yes, but it racks and tortures the spiritually re-
tarded....

And so, in YOU CAN'T TAKE IT WITH YOU, I
again tampered with drama's classic four. I combined the villain and the hero; changed Kirby, Sr.--
the play's two-dimensional, cardboard bad guy--
into the film's villain-hero.--Frank Capra (in The
Name above the Title).

YOU CAN'T TAKE IT WITH YOU is such a jumble of
tones and moods that it practically demands a like jumble of
an analysis. As with Capra's previous film, LOST HORIZON,
a more or less futile attempt has been made to force undramatic material into a dramatic structure. Undramatic
material can make a good movie, but it's hardly likely to
make good drama. In this case the hybrid is somewhat more
successful, but, though little of it can be dismissed without
qualification, none of it can be praised without qualification.

The movie goes wrong in so many ways that it's a
wonder it's any good at all, but Capra, Riskin, Edward
Arnold, James Stewart, Jean Arthur, Mischa Auer, and the
other members of the cast keep righting it, if sometimes
only for a moment. And much as I admire the initiative
Capra and Riskin evidently took in rewriting the play (which
I haven't read or seen performed and don't intend to), I think
that where the movie most seriously goes wrong is in the ex-
pansion of Arnold's role, despite his intermittently impressive
performance and the fact that he gives the movie its finest
moments. Ironically, it's when the stage is all Arnold's that
the movie is at its worst. Far from eliminating what Capra
calls the "cardboard bad guy" of the play, he and Riskin play
right into that tired variation, the cardboard-bad-guy re-
deemed. You can see the redemption coming a mile down
the track, and it's slow freight.

The movie opposes unhappy wealth with fun, daffy poverty, with nothing in-between. Its wildly different locations
are like the sets for three or four different movies. It has
no mobility, no continuity between sequences. The movie
pays for the contrivance of irreconcilable extremes with the
fatuous unreality of its conclusion, which has Anthony P. Kirby giving up his millions to play the harmonica. In only a
few instances--Alice and Tony at a cafe; the Kirbys at the
Sycamores, in a screwball version of ALICE ADAMS' fiasco
of a dinner--is there comic point to the extremes.

   With the ungainly structure and the simplistic basics
of YOU CAN'T TAKE IT WITH YOU, it might seem that
there isn't room for much else. But while it's formally dis-
integrating, informally it manages to hold together for scenes
at a time.

   The ideals of individualism embodied in the Sycamores
are pretentiously unpretentious. Grandpa plays the harmonica.
Mrs. Sycamore, his daughter, writes stories, but only because someone once accidentally delivered a typewriter to
their house. Mr. Sycamore makes firecrackers in the basement. Daughter Essie practices ballet. Her husband plays
the xylophone. Guest Kolenkhov (from Omsk) is a ballet
master and a gourmet. Guest Mr. Poppins, whom Grandpa
lures out of his job at the beginning of the movie, makes
mechanical toys and "monster" masks.

   These characters are calculated to be kookily amusing,
"irrepressible." They're conventionally unconventional. Their
forms of self-expression are more credible as comic turns
than as forms of self-expression. The philosophical import
of these scenes is appalling: these free spirits are silly
buffoons obsessed with inconsequential matters, the implicit
point being that to be free is to be a jerk. Grandpa asks
Kolenkhov how pupil Essie is progressing. "Confidentially,
she stinks!" is his answer. Grandpa replies, "Long as she's
having fun." But the movie isn't necessarily anti-art; art
simply doesn't exist in its context. Like LOST HORIZON,
YOU CAN'T TAKE IT WITH YOU is a dead-end. The struggle is over for the Sycamores and their guests. Grandpa's
savings take care of their few material needs. They exist
only to entertain themselves, and us.

   However insipid these scenes may sound, though, on
the screen they're sometimes enchanting. Basically, the
movie is as sickly as other "free spirit" comedies of the
time, such as The JOY OF LIVING, but it plays well. In-
dividually, the characters are aggressively lovable pinheads;
but as a group, as directed by Capra, they're almost a ballet
troupe. Essie is of course the première ballerina. She
sets the tone of the Sycamore sequences, which at times are
almost ethereally absurd, though not quite on the order of
the mad, incredibly intricate indoor chase of RULES OF THE
GAME. Essie spins around the dinner table as she sets it
and twirls in, right on cue, out of nowhere, camera bottom,
as Grandpa and Kirby begin their duet on the harmonicas.
Fireworks will go off in the basement at bad moments. A

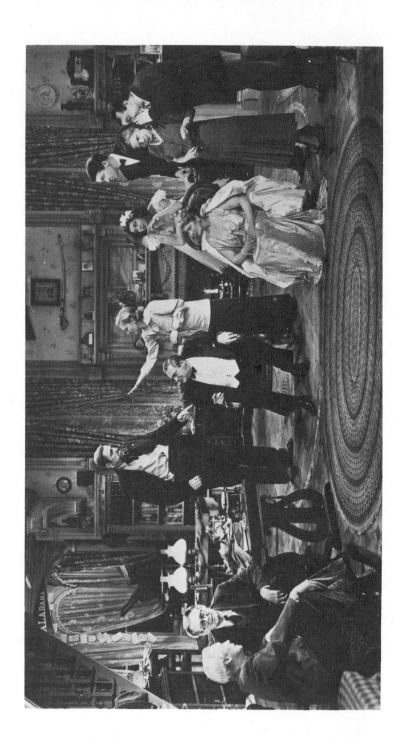

dinner plate is transformed into a "discus." Alice slides
gleefully down the bannister, figuratively right into the Kirbys. The cook (Eddie Anderson) will race through Kirbys
and Sycamores out the door, dart back in, and then run out
again ("Forgot the mustard"). Mr. Sycamore will pop up
over the cellar-stair bannister every so often like a friendly
jack-in-the-box. And Mr. Poppins enters in a new monster mask at the most inopportune times.

The Sycamore family scenes--precisely-choreographed
insanity--show what a good director can sometimes do with
mediocre, even somewhat repellent, material. (Other parts
of the movie show what usually happens.) The philosophy
of life that's so crudely expressed in the dialogue is effortlessly expressed in the staging. These scenes play well, if
they don't answer nagging questions (always in the back of
my mind as I watch them) like, Don't their shticks ever begin to bore these people? Wouldn't setting off firecrackers
all day long become as deadly dull as any menial work? Is
this really all there is to it? Is individualism being equated
with insanity? (It is, it is.) These scenes are a self-con-
tained entity--their momentum does not carry over into other
scenes, and the movie thus consists of parts which don't add
up to a whole.

The lack of continuity, of a real center for the movie,
badly fragments the performances of the principles. James
Stewart's charm will be building up all sorts of goodwill with
Jean Arthur and us when, every now and then, he'll myste-
riously drop out of the movie, for several scenes at a time.
(Stewart over-accents some small moments with Miss Arthur
but otherwise doesn't force himself.) Miss Arthur, for reasons I never can quite catch no matter how often I see the
movie, intentionally vanishes for a while after a court trial.
Edward Arnold has stage center at the Sycamores and, looking as though he has just been hit in the face with a wet fish,
he holds it in what appears to be the beginning of a strong,
comic performance. But, off by himself in his financial
prison, he waxes serious, and what happened to that other,
lighter movie?

The movie's attempt to turn Kirby, Sr. into a villain-

Opposite: YOU CAN'T TAKE IT WITH YOU - at the Sycamores', with Samuel S. Hinds, Lionel Barrymore, Mischa
Auer, Edward Arnold, Jean Arthur, Mary Forbes, Ann Miller, James Stewart, Spring Byington, Dub Taylor.

hero is a total fiasco, for several reasons. For one thing, the differences between the Kirbys and the Sycamores are exaggerated, simplistic, irreconcilable. Money precludes happiness; happiness renders money valueless. The rich have no real friends. The Sycamores are dripping with friends, who are, to put it as cynically as possible, as good as money:[1] a whole courtroom-full of them puts up the Sycamores' $100 bail at one point.

Kirby initially finds the Sycamores' social gaucherie refreshing. But Arnold's smile of delight when Mrs. Sycamore tactlessly chides his wife for her credence in occultism is the first and only convincing step towards reconciling him with the Sycamores. Kirby's conversion, to be at all convincing, would have to rely almost entirely on such moments in Arnold's performance.

Instead, things happen to Kirby like clockwork, and Arnold is rendered part of the mechanics of the plotting. Ramsey, a business associate, shows up to accuse Kirby of figuratively stabbing him in the back and promptly dies, as he says, helpfully, friendless. Even Kirby's son deserts him. All this is supposed to make Kirby's conversion look as though it's not quick or artificial. As it turns out, his conversion is just slow and artificial. The conclusion is foregone. Kirby is simply Mr. Poppins on a grander scale, and no one refuses an invitation to Shangri-La.

Must evil be thoroughly vanquished? Does everyone in a movie have to be happy to make a happy ending? Capra apparently thought so--he wanted MEET JOHN DOE to end with even D. B. Norton (Edward Arnold again) going over to the other side. I think that it was a minor mistake for the last, stubborn holdout in AMERICAN MADNESS to capitulate. Here the mistake--Kirby's conversion--is major. It's the basis of half the movie.[2] The old Anthony P. Kirby must be thoroughly discredited while, at the end, the other extreme still stands, complacent (Grandpa to Kirby: "I used to be just like you") and static.

Notes

1.   Capra's earlier AMERICAN MADNESS actually had alternate pre-release titles of FAITH and MONEY!

2.   The minor mistake of AMERICAN MADNESS is corrected:

the last holdout, Mrs. Kirby, remains skeptical of
the joys of lunacy at fade-out, though it looks as
though she's succumbing.

Chapter 8

ARSENIC AND OLD LACE

Warner Brothers. 1941 (released 1944). 118 minutes.

Director, Producer: Frank Capra. Screenplay: Julius J. and Philip G. Epstein. Based on the play by Joseph Kesselring as produced by Howard Lindsay and Russel Crouse. Photography: Sol Polito. Music: Max Steiner. Musical Director: Leo F. Forbstein. Orchestral Arrangements: Hugo Friedhofer. Art Director: Max Parker. Editor: Daniel Mandell. Special Effects: Byron Haskin, Robert Burks. Dialogue Director: Harold Winston. Makeup: Perc Westmore. Assistant Director: Russ Saunders. Gowns: Orry-Kelly. Sound: C. A. Riggs.

Cast: Cary Grant (Mortimer Brewster), Raymond Massey (Jonathan Brewster), Peter Lorre (Dr. Einstein), Josephine Hull (Abbey Brewster), Jean Adair (Martha Brewster), Edward Everett Horton (Mr. Witherspoon), Priscilla Lane (Elaine Harper), John Alexander (Teddy Brewster), Jack Carson (O'Hara), James Gleason (Lt. Rooney), Garry Owen (taxi driver), Grant Mitchell (Reverend Harper), Edward McNamara (Brophy), John Ridgely (Saunders), Vaughan Glaser (Judge Cullman), Chester Clute (Dr. Gilchrist), Charles Lane (reporter), Edward McWade (Gibbs), Leo White (man in phone booth), Spencer Charters (marriage license clerk), Hank Mann (photographer), Lee Phelps (umpire).

New York drama critic Mortimer Brewster, a newly-wed, discovers that his spinster aunts Abbey and Martha have been poisoning old men. They do not murder indiscriminately, but humanely, making sure that the victims are lonely and have no home or family. They use a mixture consisting of a gallon of elderberry wine, a teaspoonful of arsenic, a half-teaspoon of strychnine, and a "pinch of cyanide." Mortimer's honeymoon is ruined. The Brewster household also

includes the relatively harmless Teddy, who imagines himself Teddy Roosevelt and occupies himself with charging up
San Juan Hill (a staircase) and building the Panama Canal
(a cellar graveyard for Abbey and Martha's victims), and
their nephew Jonathan, a ringer for Boris Karloff/Franken-
stein's monster thanks to his aide Dr. Einstein's bungled
plastic surgery. Jonathan and the doctor arrive in the dead
of night. (Einstein is a Peter Lorre look-alike, though
nothing is ever made of this.) Jonathan has murdered an
even dozen; Aunt Abbey and Aunt Martha have twelve victims
too, and the competition is fierce when they meet. Jonathan
counts on Mortimer to put him one up on them; Abbey and
Martha gracefully bide their time, hoping for someone older,
lonelier, and unrelated to happen along. But to Jonathan's
way of thinking, Mortimer, whom he despises, should perhaps count double. Jonathan, who has less of a flair than
his aunts for disposing of bodies, stows his latest in their
window seat, the first place that anyone would look. Everyone does, and that's most of the story.

Part One

Like IT'S A WONDERFUL LIFE and MEET JOHN
DOE, Capra's ARSENIC AND OLD LACE is an old favorite
of mine from television viewings.[1] I once thought it was
the funniest movie ever made. Its spell has, however, partially faded for me. After my last TV viewing of ARSENIC
AND OLD LACE, several years ago, I attributed my disenchantment simply to over-familiarity with the material and,
halfway through, gave up on it. I figured that I must have
seen the movie something like 30 times; I had seen at least
one television version; I had read the play and memorized
lines ("Pull up a tombstone," "Insanity runs in my family.
It practically gallops!", "Not the Melbourne method!", my
favorite Peter Lorre line); and I knew the movie as well as
if I had written it myself. Last year (1972) I saw a half
hour of it again at a college screening and guessed that I
probably hadn't seen it 30 times. It just seemed as though
I had.

It's not just that Cary Grant mugs; the whole movie
mugs. The volume is set a little too high to begin with and
is never turned down, only up once in a while. Philip T.
Hartung captured the spirit: "Even in the torture scene,
with a gag over his face, Grant can express hope, fear,
cunning and a wonderful brand of amazement."[2] Grant

plays the rest of the movie without a gag over his face, but
as if there were a gag over his face. But he isn't trying to
run away with the movie. He's just trying to keep up with
it. His strenuous performance is perfectly in keeping with
the manic proceedings. Capra must have encouraged everyone to wring the material for all it was worth, and they
probably did. With this version around, no one would dare
attempt a movie remake.

There's an excess of everything. Jack Carson's and
Garry Owen's double and triple takes are predicated on the
assumption that if one actor's (Grant's) takes are funny, two
actors' takes are twice as funny, and three, three times as
funny. Even Max Steiner's music mugs. The exaggeration
and lack of discipline take their toll. Unrestraint rules,
and a single exposure to ARSENIC AND OLD LACE might,
in Pauline Kael's word (for other movies), be "liberating."
But one exposure is as good as six, and by the second you
may be ready to be liberated from being liberated. If too
much onscreen emotion can detach the viewer from a weepie,
too much frenetic clowning can take the same viewer right
out of a comedy. The movie's mugging and excess act like
the burst of a flashbulb on the retina. ARSENIC AND OLD
LACE is unforgettable, unfortunately. The damn clever lines
come back to haunt you, whether you want them to or not.

It's a black comedy, and the Brewsters are the other,
lethal side of the Sycamores, the mindless free spirits of
YOU CAN'T TAKE IT WITH YOU. Either family is guaran-
teed to give you the creeps one way or another, intentionally
or not. A perfect comedy might be made of the Brewsters'
extermination of the Sycamores (justifiable homicide) or even
from the Sycamores' bafflement of the Brewsters as the former unwittingly frustrate their murderous designs. By itself
each family is a little too strong and unadulterated; each has
it too much its own way. There's a running (or galloping)
gag in ARSENIC AND OLD LACE about committing Teddy to
Happydale, but the joke is, half-intentionally, that the Brewster residence is an undesignated insane asylum.

Part Two

I recently, finally, saw the whole movie again and I
was again almost suffocated by the familiarity of the lines
and situations. But one thing surprised me, in fact stunned
me--Cary Grant's performance. I realize that the movie is

as disreputable in critical circles as it is popular with the
public--my peculiar experience with it has enabled me to see
both sides of the issue--and that Grant's Mortimer Brewster
is not held to be one of the nobler demonstrations of the art
of acting.   (Kael: "... Grant gives one of his rare terrible
performances....") But I'm afraid I think Grant's performance is just tremendous.   In fact, I love it (though I no longer love the movie).

        Hartung thought the original play was "highly over-
rated," and, though I don't remember much from my reading
of it, I suspect that he's right.   Others have complained that
the movie's hysterics wrecked the quiet intimacy of the play's
comic horrors, but I doubt it.   It's not the dither and pother
of the movie that's monotonous.   It's that smug central con-
ceit--the two, sweet little old murderers.   Like other black
comedies about crime and violence--Hitchcock's twin disasters, The TROUBLE WITH HARRY and TO CATCH A THIEF,
HAROLD AND MAUDE, SOMETHING FOR EVERYONE--AR-
SENIC AND OLD LACE has a juvenile fascination with crime
and a complacent belief in its ability to shock and amuse
with the supposed novelty of its irreverent treatment of
crime and criminals.   Those other movies were based almost entirely on that belief and are unbearably smug.   But
ARSENIC AND OLD LACE has the major redeeming feature
of Grant's performance, the minor redeeming features of
Peter Lorre's and John Alexander's performances, and odd,
redeeming surprise (rather than, Surprise, surprise!) lines
and bits, like the bit where Teddy walks in on the seated
Jonathan and Dr. Einstein and peremptorily begins, "Gentle-
men, be seated!", and the two, in a reverse-reflex action,
rise.   If only the relentless irony of the little old sweeties
with the 12 murders not on their consciences were early
doubled back on itself, and the dears were given a little
taste of their own medicine.   The two, however, do serve
an esthetic purpose: they drive Mortimer crazy.

        Kael hit on it, but considered it the secret of the
movie's failure rather than its success.   It may be a lousy
play, but Capra turns it into a terrific vehicle for Cary
Grant, whose mad acts (he has several) are anything but
monotonous.   One of the script's basic jokes is that, though
Mortimer discovers that he isn't a Brewster (and thus is
supposedly free of the Brewster heritage of madness), he is
subject to fits of insanity.   The judge even quips, in response to a visit by Mortimer, "I may be committing the
wrong Brewster." Reviews--positive and negative--of the

movie give the false impression that Grant's performance is
one long series of zany double takes, but it is in fact quite
accomplished. It's true that he's all over the set, but he's
not substituting energy for expressiveness. All the gentle
and not-so-gentle whimsy of the aunts, of Teddy, of Jonathan, of Dr. Einstein, is fodder for his versatile mugging.
He's a fantastically witty actor and can comment on his own
overplaying without stepping out of character--as when Lorre
mumbles something as the two walk downstairs and Grant
snaps, "Stop underplaying! I can't hear you, " without missing
a beat.

          He and Capra carefully modulate Mortimer's madness.
For long stretches Grant will be almost catatonic, distracted,
muttering to himself or silently observing the situation, as in
an extended communing with himself on the stairs as the action continues below him in the front room. It's an amusing
visual conceit, to which the fact that much of that action is
mundane is irrelevant. Or he'll suddenly become maniacally
moralistic, as when, crouching threateningly, he approaches
his aunts and says, of murder, "It's wrong!" His hysterical
periods are briefer than his catatonic periods and are usually
brought on by some new revelation of the misdeeds of his
aunts or Jonathan. Or the sudden recollection of a revelation will bring him out of a trance: "Now where were we
... 12!" Only when it's Grant's turn to mouth one of the
tiresome gags about murder or Jonathan's face does he temporarily return to earth. Otherwise he does one of the most
entertaining mad numbers outside of Charles Laughton's in
ISLAND OF LOST SOULS. (Laughton too has been criticized
for the unsubtlety of his Dr. Moreau.) The role of Mortimer Brewster is a plum for Grant that allows him to do just
about anything he wants (without reason), including an un-
cannily accurate impression of Edward Everett Horton.

          Lorre's Dr. Einstein and Alexander's Teddy are also
amusing creations, but it's really a one-man show. Lorre
is at his most adorably tremulous, but he's stuck with a lot
of the cutesy-poo-crime lines. And Alexander's Teddy
Roosevelt routines amusingly punctuate the main proceedings.
(Teddy: "I'm Theodore Roosevelt." Jonathan: "I'm Wood-
row Wilson. Go to bed!") There are actually many funny
lines--most of them having nothing to do with mass murder--

_____

Opposite: ARSENIC AND OLD LACE - Peter Lorre, Raymond Massey, Jean Adair, Josephine Hull, and the window
seat.

such as Mortimer's later exchanges with the cab driver who
waits for him and leaves the meter running all through the
movie: Cabbie: "$22.50!" Mortimer (thinking he's showing
off his coat): "Oh. Yeah. Looks good on you!" Later:
"Five more bucks, and you'll own it!" Mortimer: "No,
thanks. It wouldn't fit me!" Throwaway humor like this
alternates with heavy-handed, repetitive gags about corpses
and poison, at the rate of about five, assorted gags per
minute, which means ARSENIC AND OLD LACE probably
does have more laughs--real and phony--than any other movie ever made. Most of the real laughs are Grant's.

The following, which I mention only because no one
else probably ever will, is provided as an esoteric, historical footnote. In a silent Will Rogers short called "Jubilo,
Jr." (1924), a character named "Bughouse" Bailey imagines
he's digging the Panama Canal. (This is not intended as a
slur on the inventiveness of ARSENIC AND OLD LACE.·)

Notes

1. In fact, by an odd coincidence, all of his Forties features (also including STATE OF THE UNION) and
   none of his Thirties features were early favorites of
   mine.

2. Commonweal, September 22, 1944, p. 548.

Chapter 9

A HOLE IN THE HEAD

United Artists/SinCap. 1959. 120 minutes. (GOODBYE EDEN. ALL MY TOMORROWS - pre-release titles).

Director, Producer: Frank Capra. Screenplay: Arnold Schulman. From his play, "A Hole in the Head" (originally a one-act play, "The Dragon's Head"; subsequent full-length versions titled "My Fiddle has Three Strings" and "The Heart's a Forgotten Hotel; televised as an hour-long play in 1956; novel version written concurrently with the making of the film).[1] Photography (scope, DeLuxe Color): William Daniels. Music: Nelson Riddle. Songs: "All My Tomorrows" and "High Hopes" by Sammy Cahn and James Van Heusen. Art Director: Eddie Imazu. Editor: William Hornbeck. Costumes: Edith Head. Assistant Directors: Arthur S. Black, Jr., Jack R. Berne. Make-up: Bernard Ponedel. Production Manager: Joe Cooke. Sound: Fred Lau. Hair Stylist: Helen Parrish.

Cast: Frank Sinatra (Tony Manetta), Edward G. Robinson (Mario Manetta), Eddie Hodges (Ally Manetta), Thelma Ritter (Sophie Manetta), Eleanor Parker (Mrs. Rogers), Carolyn Jones (Shirl), Keenan Wynn (Jerry Marks), Dub Taylor (Fred), Joi Lansing (Dorine), George De Witt (Mendy), Jimmy Komack (Julius Manetta), Connie Sawyer (Miss Wexler), Benny Rubin (Mr. Diamond), Ruby Dandrige (Sally), B. S. Pully (gangster), Joyce Nizzari (Alice), Pupi Campo (master of ceremonies).

Widower Tony Manetta, an irresponsible dreamer, faces foreclosure of his run-down Miami hotel. He spends his time promoting far-fetched business schemes (such as a $5-million amusement park), romancing a bongo-playing girl named Shirl, and bringing up his son, Ally. His difficulties with the hotel and Ally bring his practical, well-to-do broth-

121

er, Mario, and his wife, Sophie, from New York.   Mario,
who considers his brother a bum, wants Tony to give up the
hotel and go into something respectable.   He tries to fix him
up with a rich, respectable widow, Eloise Rogers, too.   But
Tony reveals the marriage-for-money plot to her and thus
ends it.   A promise of help from an old buddy, Jerry Marks,
proves illusory.   He finally gives up, agreeing with Mario
that he's a bum, and sends Ally off to live with Mario and
Sophie.   But Ally eludes them and returns to Tony.

A HOLE IN THE HEAD is so morose and melancholy
that it's surprising it did as well as it apparently did at the
box office.   It's sentimental, in a cheerless, gloomy way, in
part accidentally, because the lighter scenes with Tony and
Ally and with Mario and Sophie fall so flat.   It's an unpleasant movie, at its infrequent best when it tries to be unpleasant, at its more typical worst when it tries to be uplifting
and positive.   It's a weird mixture of ingredients that's at
least more interesting, if not much better, than Capra's two
previous features, the formula Paramounts.

A HOLE IN THE HEAD takes the mindless-free-spirit
idea of YOU CAN'T TAKE IT WITH YOU and tries to attack
it.   Unfortunately, the free spirits in this movie have no
real or even superficial attraction, and a film can hardly attack something that isn't there.   The movie is so determined
to demonstrate the worth of its father-son relationship that
phony awe and reverence for the joys of father-and-son-hood
paralyze it: Tony and Ally talk "man-to-man," and there
are close shots of Ally's knowing looks and self-indulgent
smiles.

The movie is an amorphous mass of feelings and
verbiage.   The characters are all talk and no action--like
the people in the film version of OF MICE AND MEN--and
their daydreams are dull.   There's a disparity between the
importance the writer and director attach to the characters'
aspirations and relationships and the importance the viewer
does.   Work (Mario) and play (Tony) seem, only partly intentionally, desiccated, unattractive alternatives.

Capra tries to inject some life into the dreary thing
by redoing a couple of old gags from his other movies--the
recalcitrant chair[2] from YOU CAN'T TAKE IT WITH YOU
(used at least five times, with one amusing variation); the
backing-up-the-stairs routine from The STRONG MAN (which
routine Capra, in his book, lamented Harry Langdon's re-

using in a later silent!). But he tries too hard and just gets
the physical effect of a sudden fall or a platform chair slap-
ping a back.

A HOLE IN THE HEAD strains to be positive, hopeful.
It finds gloom more natural, as when, near the end, Tony
lashes out at Mario, or when, his back to the camera, he
admits, "I'm nothing but a bum"--when it admits its gloom-
iness. The most interesting scene is the nightmarish conclusion to the Jerry Marks episode, in which Marks admits
that he was wise to Tony all along and that he let him go on
only because he was an old friend. It's a real shocker because, when finally the ugliness in the movie surfaces, the
movie turns out to be even uglier than it appeared to be.
In retrospect, the film might seem to have been working all
along to the stomach punch that Marks' bodyguard administers
to Tony, but there was no real indication that our dreamer-
hero was due to be that convincingly disillusioned. The
harshness of this scene (which says, emphatically, that you
don't get something for nothing) is not consonant with the
rest of the movie (which says, resignedly, that you get
nothing for nothing), even given the general unpleasantness.
Was Capra responsible for its grimness? (The whole Marks
sequence is original with the movie.)

There is, oddly, with all the hot air and self-pity,
one touching scene, neither unredeemedly harsh nor vacantly
affirmative. Tony goes to Eloise's apartment, but, when
she admits that she's serious about the prospective match,
he guiltily admits that he's there under false pretenses, to
get money out of Mario. There's no thematic design to the
movie as a whole, but here it seems no accident that while
Tony and Eloise open up to each other and find themselves
at cross-purposes, Shirl finds herself alone at the hotel,
stood up by Tony. The movie improves this scene merely
by moving it from the hotel (where it was set in the play) to
Eloise's apartment, a setting which psychologically under-
scores her emotional vulnerability.

The nadir of A HOLE IN THE HEAD is the ending.
Sophie remarks of the romping Tony, Ally, and Eloise,
"They're so happy and so poor," and Mario instructs her,
"Broke, yes, but they're not poor. We're poor"; and it's
YOU CAN'T TAKE IT WITH YOU all over again as they join
the trio.

Otherwise, the movie is generally no better or worse

than the play, a thin, less ambitious work which relies too
heavily on the intermittent charm of its Jewish dialect.

Notes

1. According to <u>Positif</u>, December 1971, p. 86, the tele-
    vision version was titled "The Heart is a Forgotten
    Hotel," directed by Arthur Penn, and shown in 1955.

2. In the play, "A Hole in the Head," it was one of those
    contortionistic "modern" chairs.

PART III

EARLY COLUMBIA, LATE PARAMOUNT COMEDIES

Chapter 10

PLATINUM BLONDE

Columbia. 1931. 82 minutes.

Director: Frank Capra. Screenplay: Jo Swerling. Continuity: Dorothy Howell. Dialogue: Robert Riskin. Based on a story by Harry E. Chandlee and Douglas W. Churchill. Photography: Joseph Walker. Technical Director: Edward Shulter. Editor: Gene Milford. Sound: Edward Bernds.

Cast: Robert Williams (Stew Smith), Jean Harlow (Anne Schuyler), Loretta Young (Gallagher), Louise Closser Hale (Mrs. Schuyler), Walter Catlett (Bingy Baker), Halliwell Hobbes (Smythe), Donald Dillaway (Michael Schuyler), Reginald Owen (Dexter Grayson), Edmund Breese (Conroy), Claude Allister (Dawson), Dick Pritchard.

Reporter Stew Smith's editor details him to get a breach-of-promise-suit story out of the Schuyler mansion. The last thing the well-to-do Schuylers want is publicity, but Smith has the nerve to phone in his story from the house telephone. In due course he saves the family from a blackmail attempt, falls in love with the Schuyler heiress, Anne, and marries her. Reluctantly, he moves into the Schuyler mansion and becomes "the husband of Anne Schuyler." He finds himself uncomfortable with the ministrations of a gentleman's gentleman and the taunts of his fellow reporters, who label him "the Cinderella man." He throws a party for all his friends while the Schuylers are away. Their return starts a near-riot, and Smith retreats to the more agreeable surroundings of a speakeasy and his old pal, Gallagher, the girl that he left behind and that, he now realizes, he has loved from the first.

Opposite: PLATINUM BLONDE - Robert Williams, Halliwell Hobbes, Jean Harlow.

PLATINUM BLONDE was Robert Williams' last movie.
He died November 3, 1931, the week it was released. If he
had lived, he would almost surely have become a major star.
Though actors generally did better under Capra's direction;
though in PLATINUM BLONDE we're probably seeing Williams at his best, his best was terrific. As reporter Stew
Smith he gives, in Andre Sennwald's words, "a vastly amusing performance."[1] He's as good with a line as Lee Tracy
or Wallace Ford in similar fast-talking-reporter roles of the
time and has more style and substance. He has a "slow" as
well as a "fast" and he makes as much of the romantic as
the comic in PLATINUM BLONDE. His sense of movement,
the expressive use of his hands, is elegant, sophisticated.
He did some stage work and at least three other films, but
his only starring role in a movie was this one.

Jean Harlow's performance is less polished than Williams'. As in the messy The SECRET SIX of the same year,
she's warm and charming, but less as an actress than as
raw material, which she was soon to refine comedically in
DINNER AT EIGHT, CHINA SEAS, LIBELED LADY, etc.,
before she too died too early. She has one or two nice bits
and a song, with Williams, on a bed.

In terms of Capra's career, PLATINUM BLONDE is
notable primarily for his exploitation of the space in the
spacious Schuyler mansion. There's a butler carried away
with echo effects, prefiguring a similar sequence in MR.
DEEDS GOES TO TOWN; a jaded Williams playing indoor
hopscotch; Williams turning to spot Miss Harlow on a tower
("That's my wife"), and a general use of the sets as a huge
board on which to play games of movement and space with
the players. This display of technical sophistication isn't
waste motion. It gives the movie the air of having been
worked out by the actors and director rather than in a script,
an effect which is more than most movies achieve.

This is not to slight Robert Riskin's apparent contribution; like Capra, he makes everyone else look better. The
story is bumpy, but his lines, as usual, are fine, particularly Smith's cracks directed at "mother" Schuyler. Best of
all: the butler's delayed afterthought of a topper to Walter
Catlett's "I have a 'seat'"; he doesn't laugh, begins to walk
away, and returns to explain: "I've heard that one."

PLATINUM BLONDE isn't as smooth and sure as it
might be, but apart from one interminable scene with Wil-

liams and Miss Harlow in a flower arbor, behind a pictur-
esque fountain (à la LADY FOR A DAY), the movie's sharpest bits are always breaking up the more ponderous moments.
When the movie founders, it's not for long.

> The worth of PLATINUM BLONDE will be principal-
> ly in digging up further admirers of the work of
> Robert Williams.... It looks like Williams, who
> has done exceedingly well in minor roles with RKO-
> Pathe,[2] has an indisputable chance of stepping a-
> head.... Always displaying a fine screen presence
> and manner, Williams quickly ingratiates himself.
> If his succeeding parts are made to fit his person-
> ality and his demeanor, it will be eggs in his cof-
> fee for this comer. That's something to watch,
> since it would be so easy to make Williams a
> sneery, too smart-cracky type.... The picture is
> with him all the way. It gives him a great break,
> and a pip scene, when after marrying the snooty
> plat done by Jean Harlow, he renounces the whole
> gang in stiff language.....--Char., Variety, Novem-
> ber 3, 1931.

> Robert Williams registers strong as the reporter.
> He's a swell actor and should build a big following.
> --Film Daily review of PLATINUM BLONDE, Sun-
> day, November 1, 1931, p. 10.

> The Film Daily congratulates Robert Williams
> whose fine acting in RKO Pathe's DEVOTION and
> Columbia's PLATINUM BLONDE ranks him as one
> of most promising newcomers to the screen--Film
> Daily, Wednesday, November 4, 1931, p. 5.

> Robert Williams, stage actor who recently came to
> Hollywood and immediately won favor by his fine
> work, died Tuesday night of peritonitis, which set
> in following an appendicitis operation last week.--
> Film Daily, Thursday, November 5, 1931, p. 2.

Notes

1. The New York Times, October 31, 1931, p. 22.

2. The COMMON LAW, REBOUND, and DEVOTION (all 1931).

Chapter 11

AMERICAN MADNESS

Columbia. 1932. 75 minutes. (FAITH. MONEY).

Director: Frank R. Capra. Story and Dialogue: Robert
Riskin. Photography: Joseph Walker. Editor: Maurice
Wright. Producer: Harry Cohn. Assistant Director: C.
C. Coleman. Sound: Edward Bernds.

Cast: Walter Huston (Thomas Dickson), Pat O'Brien
(Matt), Kay Johnson (Mrs. Dickson), Gavin Gordon (Cluett),
Constance Cummings (Helen), Robert Ellis (Dude Finlay),
Berton Churchill (O'Brien), Arthur Hoyt (Ives), Edwin Max-
well (Clark), Robert Emmett O'Connor (the inspector),
Jeanne Sorel (Cluett's secretary), Walter Walker (Schultz),
Edward Martindale (Ames), Anderson Lawlor (Charlie),
Sterling Holloway, Harry Holman.

Against strong opposition from his board of directors,
Thomas Dickson, president of the First National Bank, sticks
to his policy of making loans based on character rather than
collateral. He devotes so much time to his work that he
neglects his wife, who is left open to head cashier Cluett's
advances. Cluett has run up $50,000 in gambling debts to
gangsters, who force him to help them rob his bank. To
give himself an alibi, he arranges for Mrs. Dickson to be
at his home during the midnight robbery. Matt Brown, an
assistant cashier at First National, an ex-convict whom Dickson had trusted, has been quietly observing their affair and
surprises them at Cluett's. When Matt is accused of being
an accessory to the robbery, he cannot offer a satisfactory
alibi without involving Mrs. Dickson. News of the crime begins to spread, and rumor ups the take from $100,000 to

Opposite: AMERICAN MADNESS - Pat O'Brien, Gavin
Gordon, Kay Johnson.

$500,000 to five million dollars. A run on the bank begins.
Dickson, unable to get help from other influential banks,
goes to his directors, but they refuse to contribute their
own assets. He tries to stall depositors from withdrawing
their own assets. He tries to stall depositors from withdrawing their money by sending word to the cashiers to have
big bills changed to small ones. Meanwhile, the police trap
Cluett into confessing the truth about the robbery. Finally,
Matt begins calling up Dickson's friends and asks them to
come and deposit all they can. The odds are still against
First National until the directors, prompted by the sight of
Dickson's friends, pool their assets and raise other millions.
The bank is saved.

Some of Frank Capra's later pictures may seem, at
first glance, to exist for a single set-piece. Obviously,
AMERICAN MADNESS too can be said to exist for its set-
piece--the run on the bank (which, more for its idea of re-
ciprocal aid than for any techniques, prefigures the run in
IT'S A WONDERFUL LIFE). But AMERICAN MADNESS
justifies itself with me with a single camera movement.

Capra uses a quick, introductory pan to sum up,
rather breathtakingly, the one scene set at the head cashier
Cluett's. The camera pans to the right with Mrs. Dickson
and Cluett as they step into his front room and continues
panning right with her as she sits down at a piano and tries
it out. The camera momentarily stops with her; then, as
she spies a third party (offscreen right), it continues the pan
along her line of sight over to Matt, seated, waiting to begin his speech. Joe Walker's camera all but takes a bow
at the showy succinctness of the shot.

The movie as a whole is notable primarily for its
weird structure, in which everything eventually falls into
place, against great odds. The above shot suggests both
what's right and what's wrong with the movie. The complicated plot hardly matters--it's the silly precision with which
it's worked out that's amusing. AMERICAN MADNESS, more
than any other Capra film I've seen, qualifies as a pure
technical exercise, a successful if rather hollow one, with
the characters strictly agents of the tricky plot. Riskin apparently wrote the script in reverse, from the concluding
set-piece on back to the beginning. It's an exciting conclusion, and one could hardly blame Riskin if he sold the idea
for it to Capra and then wrote a movie to go with it. It's
as much a technical exercise for him--tying up loose ends

of the plot and maneuvering the characters toward the climactic scenes--as it is for Capra, rushing actors in and
out of fragments of scenes as the run starts and creating a
collage of panic, confusion, and contagious excitement.

At times Riskin resorts to the baldest exposition (bank
secretary, helpfully: "That's Dude Finlay--he's one of the
toughest gangsters in town"), but Capra takes up the slack
by making what amounts almost to a documentary of a bank.
This is the film with which, he says in his book, he began
to speed up the pace of scenes "to about one-third above
normal ... but when AMERICAN MADNESS hit the theater
screens, the pace seemed normal!"[1] But he also takes his
time with establishing scenes and captures the look and feel
of banking operations. He has scenes shot so as to give an
idea of the size and shape of the place, where the balconies
and alcoves are, who is where when, etc. Reviews of the
time commented on the "authenticity of the vault shots"[2] and
the "sequences devoted to the locking and unlocking of the
imposing vault."[3] Though the story is pure melodrama, the
setting is authentic, and for the climactic run all that's needed is the look of reality. The second most spectacular shot
in AMERICAN MADNESS--nothing could top that one pan--is
an extended, static, overhead view of the length of the bank's
interior quickly filling up with people as the rumors spread.

The movie has the damnedest vignettes. One of the
bank's telephone operators switches voices as handily as
lines. During the run, Matt takes over two phones at once
to talk to Dickson's friends. An employee (Sterling Holloway) describes the shooting of a bank guard ("Dead? Life-
less!") to anyone who will listen. Matt runs into trouble
trying to establish an alibi with his landlady and her clock
("When it's four, it's one").

But most of the pleasures the movie offers are incidental ones of comedy, setting, and performance. The characters just happen to be needed at the end. Dickson is often
just a mouthpiece for Capra and Riskin's socio-economic
theories. Some of his early speeches are just that--speeches,
too straight, leaving you waiting for the punch line (like his
comment at one point on the forbidding appearance of the
board members: "Seven more and you'd make a jury").
And, as Commonweal critic Richard Dana Skinner wondered,
how did this "master judge of men and character" hire someone like Cluett ("a complete swine")?[4] Gavin Gordon as
Cluett, the lady-killer, is incredible, though his creepiness

is partially intended. He does a foolish "aghast, " a silly
"weak, " and a phony "surprised. " His name (Cyril Cluett)
doesn't help either.

Matt is a victim of the machinations of the plot at its
cleverest: a reformed criminal accused of a crime, shield-
ing the guilty party and his boss's wife, he injures his em-
ployer whether he speaks up or not. A real dilemma.
(That's what comes of keeping your nose clean.) And Mrs.
Dickson is little more than the usual wife-ignored-by-husband.
The board members are stick-figure villains, and even the
chief villain among them capitulates to Dickson, unconvincingly, with a lame: "If everybody's gone crazy, I'll go crazy
too. "

As Dickson, Walter Huston is, as always, good. His
performance seems half responsible for the pace and force
of the movie. He almost makes Dickson's speeches exciting
theater. Although I don't think he was quite a great actor,
he was one of our most consistent actors. (Greater actors
are generally more erratic.) In the fourteen films I've seen
him in, he gives only one performance which I thought was
less-than-good (in D. W. Griffith's ABRAHAM LINCOLN).
(The following year, 1933, Huston made some more memorable speeches in another topical movie, GABRIEL OVER THE
WHITE HOUSE, which was really just one long speech, with
a few dramatic interludes, about a President of the United
States who becomes the country's benevolent dictator.)

Pat O'Brien's Matt Brown is good contrast to Huston's Dickson--careful, calm, deliberative, the passive to
Huston's active.

> It is one of the wastes of our age that moving pic-
> tures, which are such powerful vehicles for propa-
> ganda, have, when used for this purpose, been so
> badly handled. A recent development has been the
> production of regular blood and thunder melodramas
> that are interrupted at intervals while characters
> make moral speeches.... What is needed now is
> a movie showing that war-debt cancellation helped
> John Brown's business and made it possible for
> him to marry his beautiful Jane. --The New Repub-
> lic, commenting on AMERICAN MADNESS, August
> 31, 1932, p. 58.

Notes

1. Frank Capra, The Name above the Title (New York, 1971), p. 140.

2. Motion Picture Herald, July 9, 1932, p. 36.

3. New York Times, August 6, 1932, p. 14.

4. The Commonweal, August 17, 1932, p. 392.

Chapter 12

LADY FOR A DAY and POCKETFUL OF MIRACLES

LADY FOR A DAY. Columbia. 1933. 88 minutes. (aka
MADAME LA GIMP. BEGGARS' HOLIDAY).

Director: Frank Capra. Screenplay: Robert Riskin, based
on the short story, "Madame La Gimp" (in Guys and Dolls),
by Damon Runyon. Remade in 1961 as POCKETFUL OF
MIRACLES. Photography: Joseph Walker. Musical Director: Bakaleinikoff. Art Director: Stephen Goosson.
Editor: Gene Havlick. Costumes: Robert Kalloch. Assistant Director: C. C. Coleman. Sound: Edward Bernds.

    Cast: Warren William (Dave the Dude), May Robson
(Apple Annie), Guy Kibbee (Judge Blake), Glenda Farrell
(Missouri Martin), Ned Sparks (Happy McGuire), Jean Parker
(Louise), Walter Connolly (Count Romero), Nat Pendleton
(Shakespeare), Halliwell Hobbes (butler), Barry Norton (Car-
los), Samuel S. Hinds (the mayor), Robert Emmett O'Connor
(the inspector), Irving Bacon (dupe), Hobart Bosworth (the
governor), Wallis Clark (the commissioner), Ward Bond?

    Apple Annie, an old harridan who peddles fruit around
Times Square, secretly educates her illegitimate daughter,
Louise, in a Spanish convent. In letters to the girl written
on class-hotel paper, Annie passes herself off as Mrs. E.
Worthington Manville. With the aid of an employee of the
hotel, where she pretends to live, she receives her daughter's
answers to her letters. In the most recent one, Louise (now
seventeen) announces her engagement to the son of a Spanish
nobleman and their intention to sail to New York to meet her
before the wedding. Annie enlists the aid of Dave the Dude,
a gambler who believes that he can't win unless he buys an
apple from Annie before a big game. She wants him to help
her continue her deception in the count's presence. Dave,
in turn, calls on his mob of hoods and pool hustlers to play

society ladies and gents. He borrows a plush hotel from a
friend. His girl, Missouri Martin, with the aid of dress-
makers and beauticians, dresses Annie up to look like a
lady. Dave assigns the role of Mr. E. Worthington Manville to the Judge, in consideration of his slang-free vocabu-
lary. Despite all the preparations, complications arise when
Louise, her fiancé, and his father, Count Romero, arrive.
Dave must have inquisitive society reporters "detained," and
the disappearances arouse the police. But when Dave explains the story to officials, they and their wives attend a
reception given by Annie (as Mrs. Manville). Everything
works out happily, and Annie sees her daughter off to Spain.

POCKETFUL OF MIRACLES.   United Artists/Franton.
1961. 136 minutes. scope. Technicolor.

Director, Producer: Frank Capra.   Screenplay: Hal Kanter,
Harry Tugend; (uncredited) Jimmy Cannon.   Based on the
story, "Madame La Gimp," by Damon Runyon and on the film
LADY FOR A DAY.   Photography: Robert Bronner.   Music:
Walter Scharf.   Song: "Pocketful of Miracles" by Sammy
Cahn and James Van Heusen.   Art Direction: Hal Pereira,
Roland Anderson.   Sets: Sam Comer, Ray Moyer.   Editor:
Frank P. Keller.   Costumes: Edith Head, Walter Plunkett.
Assistant Directors: Arthur S. Black, Jr., Frank Capra,
Jr.   Choreography: Nick Castle.   Associate Producers:
Glenn Ford, Joe Sistrom.   Sound: Hugo and Charles Grenz-
bach.

        Cast: Glenn Ford (Dave the Dude), Bette Davis (Apple
Annie), Hope Lange (Queenie Martin), Arthur O'Connell
(Count Romero), Peter Falk (Joy Boy), Thomas Mitchell
(Judge Blake), Edward Everett Horton (butler), Mickey
Shaughnessy (Junior), David Brian (governor), Sheldon
Leonard (Steve Darcey), Peter Mann (Carlos), Ann-Margret
(Louise), Barton MacLane (police commissioner), John Litel
(the inspector), Jerome Cowan (the mayor), Jay Novello
(Spanish consul), Frank Ferguson and Willis Bouchey (news-
paper editors), Fritz Feld (Pierre), Ellen Corby (Soho Sal),
Gavin Gordon (hotel manager), Benny Rubin (Flyaway), Jack
Elam (Cheesecake), Mike Mazurki (Big Mike), Hayden Rorke
(Capt. Moore), Doodles Weaver (pool player), Paul E. Burns
(Mallethead), Angelo Rossitto (Angie), Edgar Stehli (Gloomy),
George E. Stone (Shimkey), William F. Sauls (Smiley), Tom
Fadden (Herbie), Snub Pollard (Knuckles), Byron Foulger,
Stuart Holmes, Kelly Thordsen, Romo Vincent.

LADY FOR A DAY is the most nearly perfect Capra film I've seen. Like Lubitsch's The SHOP AROUND THE CORNER, it's a "little" movie, an "entertainment" that completely realizes its potential. The difference between the humble ambitions of such movies and their actual accomplishments is the difference between the ordinary and art. LADY FOR A DAY is the kind of movie that gets better, and better, and better, and better, as it goes along, and when it's over you can't really say just how good it was. And it lacks the helpful flaws of Capra's later films and thus makes analysis either impossible or very simple, depending on what you think an analysis of a movie should be. LADY FOR A DAY's near-perfection makes discussion of it like examination of a watch that keeps perfect time. The watchmaker can only somewhat superfluously take it apart and try to put it back together again. Capra, Riskin, Cohn--everyone made the right decisions. There's nothing to correct or suggest in retrospect.

Such total success in a movie doesn't encourage speculative meddling with its ingredients. Jean Parker's filial devotion might seem overstressed. Or, perhaps, Nat Pendleton is expendable--Ned Sparks, Guy Kibbee and Glenda Farrell, one might reasonably argue, are enough to keep the story light and funny. Or perhaps May Robson needn't be so shrilly fearful of being exposed as a fraud. On the other hand, Misses Parker and Robson must make their presences felt somehow. And I, personally, could not do without Nat Pendleton as Shakespeare--at least not without the bit when, after babbling on unbidden, he complies with Warren William's "Shut up!" with "I was just gonna do dat." One might ask for more of each ingredient. But Capra and Riskin correctly calculated what should go in and they probably also calculated just how much should go in.

I don't think there's any single key to the success of LADY FOR A DAY; there are several. The most obvious is the story. From a wisp of a premise (Damon Runyon's little sketch), Capra and Riskin fashioned a feature-length, short-story movie, which term should be but isn't a contradiction. They embellished the original, which was somewhat slender even for a short story, and made something similar to, but more substantial than, a short story. The key to this key is that they didn't expand Runyon's story, but simply fleshed it out with characters and situations. They didn't overextend it. They accepted the structural limits of the Runyon original and rewrote it into a consistently imaginative, inventive com-

edy-drama. They apply, to a slight, serio-comic premise,
the silent-comedy principle of building and find more in it
than anyone would have thought possible; and, while LADY
FOR A DAY isn't as funny as Capra's best silent comedy,
The STRONG MAN, by the end it's genuinely affecting, which
The STRONG MAN never is.[1]

There really aren't that many movies that could stand
on the strength of their stories, but LADY FOR A DAY is
an example of superlative storytelling. Capra and Riskin
keep the developments cascading. The movie leaps from one
complication to another, not haphazardly but logically, developing the potential of the premise and never straying or
stalling. Each new complication is an extension of that lady-
for-a-day premise, arising naturally out of previous extensions. But it's not so much the ingeniousness of the complications as the beauty with which they're resolved that
makes LADY FOR A DAY an almost perfect modern-day
fairy tale.

The term "fairy tale" implies pleasant resolutions.
Unlike most art forms, the fairy tale deals in answers, not
questions, and LADY FOR A DAY seems inspired whenever
it has to come up with an answer. Dave the Dude has his
most unfriendly-looking thugs surround the party from Spain
at the dock so that curious reporters can't get near. Public
officials order the reporters kidnapped by Dave to say that
they were out on a drunk. And it might have been enough
for the Judge simply to win the billiards match with the
Count or for Dave's mob to show up at Annie's reception.
But enough isn't enough. The Judge wins with a miracle
shot and departs the room before it's finished, leaving Count
Romero in stunned awe to run after him to tell him he has
won. And the governor and the mayor, not Harry the Horse
and Cheesecake, make the reception a dream come true.

I keep saying "nearly perfect" because the basis of
the movie is, after all, an old lady's attempt to impersonate
a society matron ... in order to impress her illegitimate
daughter ... who is traveling all the way from Spain ... with
her highborn fiancé and his father--a count! The script,
however, accepts without embarrassment the airy absurdity
of the situation and develops it rather than the pathos of it,
though without ever making fun of that situation. The script
in fact, by both acknowledging the absurdity of Annie's im-
personation and not questioning the necessity for it--by making a stunt of it yet not ridiculing it--ultimately has it both

ways.

May Robson's and Jean Parker's scenes consume relatively little running time and are handled believably, if a little "tastefully." They don't invite outright audience rejection.
This initial suspension of disbelief is crucial to later scenes,
when the story, wholly unpredictably, begins to seem very
much worth the telling, and the potential weakness of the
premise is long-forgotten, dissolved in the story's strengths,
like an unpromising little bud blossoming into a fine flower.
What seemed expendable and even potentially embarrassing
at the beginning is indispensable and even touching at the end.
The scene in which a drunken, sentimental Annie writes a
letter to her daughter is perhaps the necessary first, faltering step toward the moment when a resplendent, fulfilled
Annie nearly faints before the mayor and the governor. The
movie's good-natured wisecracking doesn't supplant sentiment
so much as nourish it, by providing an atmosphere in which
it can grow, surely but unobtrusively. Another key to the
success of LADY FOR A DAY may be that it's hard to tell
which, of the warmth and the wise-guy sarcasm, exists for
which.

One key is definitely the conception of the movie as
a team effort, with no real stars and with everyone contributing to the overall effect. Everyone is a co-star. The roles
are so well cast, and the characters are so well imagined,
that the story seems to take shape from their various attitudes toward the fairy tale--from Missouri Martin's cheerful
complicity in the scheme, to Dave's reluctant belief in what
he's doing ("I'll hang before I let you give me the horse
laugh"), to the Judge's obvious, barely contained pleasure at
being part of a plot not unlike one of his own flimflams, to
Happy's aggressive skepticism, to Annie's noisy desperation,
to Shakespeare's brute persistence. No one is expendable.

The first time I saw the movie I thought that Dave the
Dude was more or less extraneous; that he was only, in a
mechanical sense, the prime mover of the plot; that he put
it into operation and then in effect disappeared. But each of
my subsequent viewings reveals him more and more to be
the key to the key of teamwork. He reconciles the others'
diverse attitudes. He detests Missouri's emotional sloppi-
ness--kissing is just an annoyance to him--and recoils from
Annie's blessing. Yet he wonderingly admits to Happy that
he "got quite a bang out of" situating Annie in the Marberry
Hotel and establishing the Judge as her husband. And, after

initial hesitation, he's pleased when Annie forcibly pulls him
further into the plot by declaring him, before the Count and
company, an uncle of Louise.   His cautiousness and reserve
conceal and check his relish of his elaborate reworking of
"Cinderella," but the reserve is as essential as the enjoy-
ment.

LADY FOR A DAY - Jean Parker, Guy Kibbee, May Robson,
Warren William, Glenda Farrell

     Robert Riskin's contribution, in story, dialogue, and
casting--Glenda Farrell was his girl friend at the time--to
LADY FOR A DAY was evidently enormous.   However the
credit should be split between Riskin, Capra, and the cast,
the movie is about 90 per cent theirs and 10 per cent Runyon's.   The original story bears little resemblance to LADY
FOR A DAY and less to POCKETFUL OF MIRACLES.   There
are no characters, just good names for characters--Death
House Donegan, Guinea Mike, Wild William Wilkins, etc.

The novelty of the Broadway idiom carries what little there
is to the story until the payoff, a reception with an influx of
hoods and molls introduced as celebrities: "Then I hear,
'Mister Al Jolson, ' and in comes nobody but Tony Bertaz-
zola, from the Chicken Club ... 'Sophie Tucker, ' and 'Theda
Bara, ' and 'Jeanne Eagels, ' and 'Helen Morgan, ' and 'Aunt
Jemima'...." (The difference in the respective receptions
in story and movie suggests how Riskin and Capra transformed the material from comedy to comic fairy tale.) A
few of Riskin's lines for the verbal duels between Happy and
Missouri and Happy and the butler originate in the story, but
most of them are his own ideas. A sentence in Runyon
("... look like a lady ...") becomes: Missouri: "Say, when
they get through with her she's gonna look every bit as good
as me." Happy: "The idea is to make her look like a lady."
The judge (as Mr. E. Worthington Manville) amends his reaction to the Count's mention of a dowry from a mumbled,
"You kind of crept up on me with that one, " to "I wasn't
quite prepared for this. "

    Happy and Dave are ushered into the presence of some
particularly unsusceptible-looking politicians, and Happy nee-
dles him, "Ask them if they believe in fairy tales. " In perhaps the funniest scene, Happy, for no reason at all, rudely
accosts the butler (Halliwell Hobbes, the butler in PLATI-
NUM BLONDE too) and asks for Dave, introducing himself
as "Happy McGuire, the apple of his eye, that's who. Got
that straight?" "Yes, sir, I have it." Happy: "Don't let
it upset you. Four out of five have it. " On his way out,
the butler adds, "I promise not to be depressed, sir. "
(Riskin always let butlers have the last word.)

    Perhaps it's the context, but even the one "mood"
scene in LADY FOR A DAY, in which the young lovers flit
by, phantom-like, in the foreground and then camp behind a
fountain, seems romantic, exquisite, not like the prosaic
scene in PLATINUM BLONDE which corresponds to it. (Then
again, perhaps it's the background music, lifted from the
conclusion of The BITTER TEA OF GENERAL YEN.) And
the abrupt ending is forgivable, even preferable here, as it
is not in MR. SMITH GOES TO WASHINGTON. The resolution of the various strands of plot is left implicit, and, since
it is a fairy tale, we can assume the happiest resolutions.
Since Capra and Riskin were so fast with answers earlier,
it doesn't seem as though they just finally ran out of them,
as it seemed Capra and Buchman did in MR. SMITH.

The synopsis of LADY FOR A DAY serves well enough (all too well) for POCKETFUL OF MIRACLES, which adds some gags for Peter Falk, a big-time-hood role for Sheldon Leonard, and a song, uncalled for, for Ann-Margret. (It is really just not appreciated.) Hal Kanter and Harry Tugend must have liked the original movie, they copied so much and changed so little. They just diluted it. The added running time tells the story: from 88 minutes to 136 minutes. The remake, though, is not disastrously worse than LADY FOR A DAY (as YOU CAN'T RUN AWAY FROM IT is disastrously worse than IT HAPPENED ONE NIGHT). It just wholeheartedly embraces the weaknesses inherent in the material, weaknesses which the original converted into strengths.

Pleasant as it generally is, POCKETFUL OF MIRACLES is almost unwatchable if seen right after LADY, it's so similar in outline. They're like two performances of the same play, with the same director, and it's discouraging to see Capra re-do something like the Judge's spectacular pool routine and louse up the timing and staging. (That Thomas Mitchell's show of self-confidence is less sure than Guy Kibbee's doesn't help either.) Other gags are shot and cut as well as they were in LADY. But, either way, the similarities cheapen the remake--the play has already been beautifully recorded on film. Capra might have justified his remake with variant routines and sequences, as Hitchcock justified his remake of The MAN WHO KNEW TOO MUCH, but most of the additional material is weak.

Capra expands the Apple Annie role for Bette Davis, in terms of running time if not material, and raucously sentimentalizes rather than soft-pedals it. Miss Davis is good, perhaps better in the role than Miss Robson, but the damage is done by playing up the pathos. Glenn Ford is perhaps as good as Warren William but, like Apple Annie, Dave the Dude is now a starring role, and the added emphasis on it further attenuates the material. (It's almost as thin as in the Runyon story.) Hope Lange is nothing, appropriately, in a nothing role. (She mainly throws things.) The one real delight of the movie is Peter Falk, in the movie role for which he is probably best known--Joy Boy, the counterpart of Ned Sparks' Happy. His breezy, rapid-fire delivery is a suitable replacement for Sparks' acerb, Walter Matthau nasality. He alone is a reminder of the (near-) perfection of LADY FOR A DAY.

Note

1. This leads me to the Agee-like seeming contradiction
    that, while I guess maybe The STRONG MAN is bet-
    ter, I think I like LADY FOR A DAY more.   At any
    rate, I think LADY is one of Capra's four best mov-
    ies, along with The STRONG MAN, MEET JOHN DOE
    and IT'S A WONDERFUL LIFE.   And MR. SMITH
    GOES TO WASHINGTON is probably his fifth-best.
    (I believe Capra thinks it's his second-best, after
    WONDERFUL LIFE.)

Chapter 13

IT HAPPENED ONE NIGHT

Columbia. 1934. 105 minutes. (NEW YORK-MIAMI - French title).

Director: Frank Capra. Screenplay: Robert Riskin, from the short story, "Night Bus," by Samuel Hopkins Adams. Photography: Joseph Walker. Musical Director: Louis Silvers. Art Director: Stephen Goosson. Producer: Harry Cohn. Editor: Gene Havlick. Costumes: Robert Kalloch. Assistant Director: C. C. Coleman. Sound: Edward Bernds. One of the ten greatest films--Louis Marcorelles, Sight and Sound poll of critics, 1962.

Cast: Clark Gable (Peter Warne), Claudette Colbert (Ellie Andrews), Walter Connolly (Alexander Andrews), Roscoe Karns (Oscar Shapeley), Alan Hale (Danker), Ward Bond and Ed Chandler (bus drivers), Jameson Thomas (King Westley), Harry Holman (auto camp manager), Maidel Turner (manager's wife), Irving Bacon (station attendant), Wallis Clark (Lovington), Arthur Hoyt (Zeke), Blanche Friderici (Zeke's wife), Charles C. Wilson (Joe Gordon), Charles D. Brown(e) (reporter), Harry C. Bradley (Henderson), Harry Todd (flag man), Frank Yaconelli (Tony), Henry Wadsworth (drunken boy), Claire McDowell (mother); Ky Robinson, Frank Holliday, James Burke, Joseph Crehan (detectives), Mickey Daniels (vendor), Oliver Eckhardt (Dykes), George Breakston (boy), Bess Flowers (secretary), Rev. Neal Dodd (minister), Edmund Burns (best man), Ethel Sykes (maid of honor), Tom Ricketts (old man), Eddie Kane (radio announcer), Eva Dennison (society woman), Fred Walton (butler), Matty Rupert (newsboy), Milton Kibbee and Sherry Hall (reporters), Earl Pingree and Harry Hume (policemen); Ernie Adams, Kit Guard, Billy Engle, Allen Fox, Marvin Loback, Dave Wengren, Bert Starkey, Rita Ross, Kate Morgan, Rose May, Margaret Reid, Sam Josephson, Ray Creighton, John Wallace, Mimi Lindell, Blanche Rose, Jane Tallent, Charles Wilroy,

Patsy O'Byrne, Harry Schultz, Bert Scott, Emma Tansey,
Marvin Shector, William McCall and S. S. Simon (bus passengers).

    To spite her father, heiress Ellie Andrews has mar-
ried (in name only) dashing young King Westley. Her father
keeps them apart by holding her a virtual prisoner on his
yacht, where Ellie goes on a hunger strike. She manages to
escape from her cabin and leaps overboard. Later, on her
way by bus from Miami to New York, she meets Peter Warne,
a newspaperman out of a job and broke. When her suitcase
is stolen, Peter helps her out financially. They share the
discomforts of a long-distance bus ride, hitchhiking, tourist
camps, and meals consisting of raw carrots. Mr. Andrews
meanwhile searches for his daughter by plane. Ellie and
Peter fall in love. One night, while she sleeps, he races
off to his editor for $1,000 for his story on her. He plans
to use the money to get Ellie and him started right together.
When, upon waking, she discovers that he has apparently
sold her out for a story, she returns to her husband and her
father, who insists on a proper church wedding for them.
Her father finds out from Peter that he really loves her.
He communicates this information to his daughter. At the
last minute, she flees the wedding ceremony to marry Peter.

    That IT HAPPENED ONE NIGHT is the only picture
that ever won the top three Academy Awards--best picture,
actor, and actress--gives the movie an aura of glamour that
belies its slightness and unpretentiousness. With all the
blockbusters, epics, and multi-Oscar winners that Hollywood
has produced, this nice little comedy is still the only film
ever to take the Oscar triple crown! Strictly in terms of
Capra's career, IT HAPPENED ONE NIGHT doesn't seem as
important as, say, LADY FOR A DAY, the year before,
which was his first big hit, or MR. DEEDS GOES TO TOWN,
two years later, which, structurally and thematically, prefigures his major later works. Its significance as a pro-
genitor of screwball comedy is questionable. For one thing
it seems too mild, sane, and quiet to be considered screwball, though it does have an eccentric heiress, a prime ingredient of screwball comedy. [1] There's nothing wrong with
it, apart from perfunctory meanwhile-back-at-the-Daily-Globe
scenes. It's just that it's so unadventurous, so "easy," so
"safe." It doesn't employ Capra's talents for staging scenes
or "building" a film to their fullest. It's smoother than
those major later works, less flawed, but less exciting and

adventurous.

The smoothness and suppleness that limit IT HAP-
PENED ONE NIGHT are also its prime qualities.   It should
have been just another feature-length situation comedy--that
is, in lesser hands, it would have been.   But the teamwork
of Clark Gable and Claudette Colbert elevate it to successful
light romantic comedy.   It's an actor's film in the sense
that, whatever went into it, everything finally rides on the
playing of the two principles.   The appeal of the movie lies
in its reasonableness, the smooth, closely-observed inter-
action of Gable and Miss Colbert, the easy development of
character that makes the situations seem appropriately secondary and that disguises the episodic nature of the plot.   Capra
gives the actors time to work themselves naturally through
scenes.   They seem to make their own decisions, to decide
the course of the plot.

Miss Colbert's naturally, unconsciously superior attitude acts subtly on Gable's gruff indifference, and his off-
hand, sometimes blunt gallantry acts on her, and neither
realizes the effect that his or her actions has on the other.
Although they start off on the wrong foot, there's never any
terrible dissonance between the two.   They just don't know
each other, and the movie extends the romantic-comedy convention of getting acquainted over its whole length.

I suspect that Claudette Colbert was the operative element, as she was in the charming romantic comedy-drama
I COVER THE WATERFRONT (1933), which similarly combined the gruff and the sweet.   (Colbert: "Summer nights,
when the sun goes down and all the lights come out on the
docks." Ben Lyon: "And summer days, when the sun comes
up and starts to work on the fish left lying around.") She
has an adorably vacant way of concentrating on one thing at
the expense of another, as when her face falls glumly blank
as she reluctantly eats a raw carrot or when she sobs happily in the midst of despair, "Oh, he's marvelous!" Otis
Ferguson thought Gable "the outstanding feature, managing
to be a rowdy and a perfect gentleman and a newspaperman
and a young lover, all in the same breath and the most
breezy and convincing manner imaginable."[2]   Some processes
at work in movies, however, are more secret than not, and
the best anyone can do is offer guesses at their nature.[3]
At any rate, scenes with only one of the two stars or without
both point to the contrivance that IT HAPPENED ONE NIGHT
might have been.

With all the effort directed toward making events flow naturally and believably, the best and funniest sequence is the one "unrealistic" one, the hitchhiking sequence. It's deservedly celebrated, for the way it reduces Gable from complete confidence in his all-thumbs, three-point hitchhiking technique--1. "Independence--you don't care whether they stop or not." 2. "Smile--you've got a brand new story about the farmer's daughter." 3. "Pitiful--when you're broke and hungry."--to wilted resignation in a matter of minutes, and for Miss Colbert's punctuating demonstration of an alternate, highly effective, entirely thumb-less method ("... the limb is mightier than the thumb"). It's the lone example in the movie of the way to build a gag and then to top it.

Gable tries method no. 1 ("a short, jerky movement") on a solitary car and fails. (Colbert, nastily: "I still got my eye on the thumb.") He uses no. 2 ("a little wider movement") on the next car. ("When you get to 100, wake me up.") No. 2 fails. A third car immediately behind the second throws Gable off balance, and no. 3 ("a long, sweeping movement") fails. Before he can recover, another car swoops by (between him and the camera), then another, and another--a whole army of cars out of nowhere on a lonely country road--exhausting his repertoire (no. 6, no. 3, no. 12, no. 81). He finally just thumbs his nose at the last in defiant defeat. He doesn't just fail--his defeat is unreasonable, grossly unfair, overwhelming, and swift. It's not a didactic lesson on overconfidence; the punishment is comically all out of proportion to the crime.

The other famous sequence, the "walls of Jericho," is more in keeping with the reasonable tone, the fabric, of the film. It's amusing, but not really worth describing in any detail. It advances a lot more plot than might be considered wise for one sequence to advance, but it does it uninsistently, without collapsing into pure exposition. After Gable synopsizes it, Riskin has him openly acknowledge the tenuousness of the plot (Gable's and the movie's) to deliver Colbert to Jameson Thomas while Gable writes up a "day-to-day account" of her story: "That's my whole plot in a nutshell, a simple story for simple people." The sequence is notable primarily for Colbert's sarcastic outraged morality: Gable, quite practically he thinks, hangs a blanket over a tightrope to separate their cabin beds. Colbert comments drily, "That, I suppose, makes everything quite all right."

The movie's romantic elements--the steady rain which keeps Gable and Colbert together in the cabin; the moonlit country stream, the mist, and the hay as they flee the bus and Roscoe Karns; the trumpet call, the falling blanket, and the darkness in the last scene--these romantic elements stay in the background, unlike the arbor in PLATINUM BLONDE which takes over the movie. The final scene is in discreet long shot. Effects such as Miss Colbert's train billowing out behind her as she escapes the climactic wedding ceremony emerge naturally from the story and from the general atmosphere--on the bus, at the camp/motel, on the road-- of camaraderie and freedom. Long before Gable and Colbert begin to speak of love there's an ambience of openness and renewal conducive to romance.

YOU CAN'T RUN AWAY FROM IT, Columbia's 1956 remake of IT HAPPENED ONE NIGHT, manages the not inconsiderable feat of duplicating and somehow wrecking just about every scene in the original. In a gallant attempt to justify itself, it uses scope and color and it switches the romantic couple from the right side of the bus to the left side. Characters like Karns' masher ("I was just trying to make things pleasant") and Alan Hale's highway robber, who were amusingly offensive in the original, are only offensive in the remake. The spontaneous singing on the bus in the first version mutates into ridiculous musical numbers in the second, with a tune for each of the big scenes: "Howdy" for the bus, "Temporarily" for the walls of Jericho, and "Thumbin' a Ride." (It may sound as if a spoof of IT HAPPENED ONE NIGHT was intended, but it wasn't, it wasn't.) The songs are rhyming lines with no spirit. There's hardly a "right" moment in it, except for Jack Lemmon's thoughts on love, which constitute the only worthwhile scene, as good as or better than the comparable scene in the earlier film. (Unfortunately, if predictably, a reprise of the title tune immediately engulfs Lemmon's musing.) Lemmon begins the movie as if he were playing a character totally alien to himself: there's a noticeable gap between actor and role. He's better later when he's not trying to be unpleasant, but even at the end, he and June Allyson have miles to go before they come near matching the give-and-take of Gable and Colbert. It's not verifiable of course, but most remakes seem to be intentionally horrendous.

Notes

1. The more raucous TWENTIETH CENTURY of the same
    year seems more firmly in the tradition. I think of
    IT HAPPENED ONE NIGHT as romantic comedy.
    Capra's later (1938) YOU CAN'T TAKE IT WITH YOU
    might be defined as screwball comedy-drama.

2. The Film Criticism of Otis Ferguson, ed. Robert Wilson
    (Philadelphia, 1971), p. 34.

3. IT HAPPENED ONE NIGHT invariably throws critics:
    both reviews in the American Film Criticism (1972,
    Stanley Kauffmann, ed.) collection end on a note of
    baffled awe. Otis Ferguson complained that we have
    no "way of describing whatever it is that makes first-
    rate entertainment what it is." William Troy of The
    Nation concluded: "Beyond a certain point the mind
    is forced to bow down before its own inability to un-
    ravel and put together again all the parts of the
    shining and imponderable whole with which it is deal-
    ing."

Chapter 14

BROADWAY BILL and RIDING HIGH

BROADWAY BILL. Columbia. 1934. 90 minutes.
(STRICTLY CONFIDENTIAL - British title).

Director: Frank Capra. Screenplay: Robert Riskin; (un-
credited) Sidney Buchman. From a story by Mark Hellinger.
Remade in 1950 as RIDING HIGH. Photography: Joseph
Walker. Editor: Gene Havlick. Producer: Harry Cohn.

Cast: Warner Baxter (Dan Brooks), Myrna Loy (Alice
Higgins), Walter Connolly (J. L. Higgins), Lynne Overman
(Happy McGuire), Raymond Walburn (Colonel Pettigrew),
Clarence Muse (Whitey), Margaret Hamilton (Edna), Douglas
Dumbrille (Eddie Morgan), Helen Vinson (Margaret), George
Meeker (Henry Early), Jason Robards (Arthur Winslow),
Helen Flint (Mrs. Early), Helen(e) Millard (Mrs. Winslow),
Harry Holman (rube), Charles Levison [Charles Lane] and
Ward Bond (Morgan's henchmen), Edmund Breese (judge),
Harry Todd (Pop Jones), George Cooper (Joe), Charles C.
Wilson (Collins), Paul Harvey (James Whitehall), Edward
Tucker (Jimmy Baker), Frankie Darro (Ted Williams, Dan's
jockey), Bob Tansill (Whitehall's jockey), Clara Blandick
(Mrs. Peterson), Inez Courtney (Mae), Claude Gillingwater
(J. P. Chase), James Blakeley (interne), Alan Hale (orches-
tra leader), Lucille Ball?, Forrester Harvey (trainer),
Charles Middleton (veterinary), Irving Bacon (hot dog stand
owner), Pat O'Malley, Jack Mulhall, John Ince (mayor),
Herman Bing (waiter), Edward Keane (headwaiter), Kit Guard
(cab driver), Edmund Burns, Stanley Blystone (jailer), Bess
Flowers (secretary), Ernie Adams (patient), Frank McGrath
(Mr. Baxter's stand-in).

Horse-trainer Dan Brooks marries into the family of
tycoon J. L. Higgins. He operates the Higgins paper box
factory at a loss for two years before deciding to return to

151

the race track. He takes his horse, Broadway Bill, and his
stableboy, Whitey, with him. At the track he runs into old
buddies Happy, the Colonel, and others. Problems prolif-
erate for Dan. On his first test, Bill, unused to the ways
of the track, runs away. Dan tries to stall off the sheriff,
who wants to claim the horse for unpaid feed bills. He must
care for his sister-in-law Alice, who has followed him to
the track. And on the eve of the derby, rain, seeping
through the stable roof, gives Bill a cold. But applications
of mind-over-matter theory bring the horse around, and he
is finally ready to face the starter in the $25,000 handicap.
Thanks to the Colonel and Happy, inside gossip drives the
odds on Broadway Bill down from 100 to 6 to 1. Fighting
for his head against a jockey in league with gamblers, Bill
just manages to nose out the favorite--only to somersault
over, dead, at the finish. He is buried on the track where
he ran his epic race. Back in Higginsville, Dan's wife has
divorced him, and Higgins has sold off his enterprises. The
family is gathered for a final meeting when rocks crash
through the windows. Alice senses that it's Dan and rushes
out to meet him. Her father follows her, at last approving
of Dan and his vagabond ways.

RIDING HIGH. Paramount. 1950. 112 minutes.

Director, Producer: Frank Capra. Screenplay: Robert
Riskin, from a story by Mark Hellinger and the film BROAD-
WAY BILL. Additional Dialogue: Melville Shavelson, Jack
Rose. Photography: George Barnes, Ernest Laszlo. Musi-
cal Director: Victor Young. Songs: "Sunshine Cake," "The
Horse Told Me," "Sure Thing," "Some Place on Anywhere
Road" by Johnny Burke and James Van Heusen. Vocal Ar-
rangements: Joseph J. Lilley; associate: Troy Sanders.
Art Directors: Hans Dreier, Walter Tyler. Set Decora-
tions: Emile Kuri, Sam Comer. Editor: William Horn-
beck. Costumes: Edith Head. Makeup: Wally Westmore.
Assistant Director: Arthur S. Black. Process Photography:
Farciot Edouart. Sound: John Cope, Hugo Grenzbach.

        Cast: Bing Crosby (Dan Brooks), Coleen Gray (Alice
Higgins), Charles Bickford (J. L. Higgins), Frances Gifford
(Margaret Higgins), William Demarest (Happy McGuire),
Raymond Walburn (Prof. Pettigrew), James Gleason (racing
secretary), Ward Bond (Lee), Clarence Muse (Whitey), Percy
Kilbride (Pop Jones), Harry Davenport (Johnson, butler),
Margaret Hamilton (Edna), Paul Harvey (Whitehall), Douglas

Dumbrille (Eddie), Gene Lockhart (J. P. Chase), Marjorie
Hoshelle (Mrs. Early), Marjorie Lord (Mrs. Winslow), Rand
Brooks (Henry Early), Willard Waterman (Arthur Winslow),
Irving Bacon (hamburger man), Joe Frisco (comic), Frankie
Darro (Williams, jockey), Charles Lane (Erickson), Dub Tay-
lor (Joe), Oliver Hardy (horse player), Max Baer (Bertie),
Fritz Feld (couturier), Byron Foulger (maitre d'), Percy
Helton (pawnbroker), Dorothy Neumann (Dan's secretary),
Roger Davis (butler), Victor Romito (barber), Margaret
Field (maid), Richard Kipling (jailer), Edgar Dearing and
Jim Nolan (deputies), Ann Doran (nurse), Garry Owen (Har-
ry), Tom Fadden (Whitehall's trainer), Stanley Andrews (vet-
erinary), Ish Kabibble, Donald Kerr, Wilbur Mack, Gerry
Ganzer, Snub Pollard, Ed Randolph, Charles Sullivan, Laura
Elliot(t), Bob Evans.

(The plot of RIDING HIGH is the same, mutatis mu-
tandis, as the plot of BROADWAY BILL.)

Until you see RIDING HIGH and HERE COMES THE
GROOM, you can't fully understand the bitterness with which
Capra, in his book, describes his role in the sale of Liberty
Films to Paramount. Of all the Capra features I've seen,
these two Paramounts are easily the worst, the only really
bad ones. (I imagine some of those prehistoric Columbias
that I haven't seen are pretty awful too.) What's most dis-
maying about them is that there's hardly a trace of Frank
Capra. There's nothing in them to connect them with the
man who made LADY FOR A DAY or MR. SMITH GOES TO
WASHINGTON or even honest failures like LOST HORIZON.
It's as if that man never existed, as if "Paramount" directed
RIDING HIGH and HERE COMES THE GROOM. They're not
bad Capra movies; they're bad movies that Capra, rather
than Paramount lackeys like Hal Walker or Norman Taurog
happened to direct, movies that they might as well have directed.

Capra himself says that he was born to function best
"as a free man." His two Paramounts show that, constrained
by studio, script, and star, he couldn't function at all. They
were made for the Bing Crosby market of 1950-51 and no
doubt served their purpose. They're a perishable commodity,
and, like nine out of ten studio jobs, are worthless now.
There's a joke near the end of HERE COMES THE GROOM
about television--"This is better than television!"--but the
joke is that the movie is no better than bad TV situation
comedy.

RIDING HIGH, of all movies, stirred up some controversy when Manny Farber accused Capra and the film of condescending to black actor Clarence Muse's character, Whitey. Farber must have been watching the movie cross-eyed and standing on his head, trying to make something newsworthy of the failure of Capra's latest picture. Muse's displays of "unctuous love" must be in some other movie, because in this one he's just another actor, stuck in formula comedy-drama muck and making the best of a bad situation. He's actually less of a type than most of the other characters. The movie's crime is not, as Farber says, that it "eulogizes" the rich, that it does in effect the opposite of what it intended to do, but that it does nothing. It was just a waste of everyone's time, talent, and money.

RIDING HIGH, like HERE COMES THE GROOM, could more credibly be accused of misogyny. Coleen Gray's and Frances Gifford's roles are as sorry as Jane Wyman's and Alexis Smith's in the other movie. As Dan Brooks, horse lover, Crosby ignores Miss Gray through most of the movie and only belatedly turns to her in order to give the story a happy ending. The pathos of her little-girl crush on Crosby is at its most acute when she burns a chicken meant for him and bursts into tears. Miss Gifford, as Crosby's dull, repressive fiancée, won't let him wear loud socks and bemoans her fate with lines like, "People are saying I have a horse for a rival." Actually there's no competition. Crosby is obsessed with his horse, and the movie is at its unintentional funniest when it eulogizes Broadway Bill at the end: "... he not only overcame the speed of his brother horses, but he had to overcome the greed in us human beings, and we should all feel humble and a little ashamed that a horse should teach us such a lesson in honesty." Bill is supposed to be an overnight legend, but the dialogue reduces him to an idiotically misplaced moral fable.

The movie doesn't do wonders for Crosby either. He's just dull as Dan. As Farber says, his character is more a spoiled brat than a rebel against high society. He's as unpleasant in his highhandedness with them as Miss Gifford, Charles Bickford, Rand Brooks, and Willard Waterman are in theirs with him, only he's unintentionally unpleasant.

William Demarest's gloomy sarcasm is occasionally amusing opposite Crosby's cheery, buck-up-kid obliviousness. (Demarest's spitting out his champagne in a posh restaurant is perhaps the movie's finest moment. It's an old gag, but

worthy of revival.   The movie needed a lot more champagne.)
Harry Davenport has moments.   And Percy Kilbride's in-
sistent old codger is almost an original character.   But it's
Crosby's movie, and he can have it.

Chapter 15

HERE COMES THE GROOM

Paramount. 1951. 113 minutes. (YOU BELONG TO ME).

Director, Producer: Frank Capra. Screenplay: Virginia Van Upp, Liam O'Brien, Myles Connolly, from a story by Robert Riskin and O'Brien. Photography: George Barnes. Musical Director: Joseph J. Lilley. Songs: "Misto Christofo Columbo," "Your Own Little House," and "Bonne Nuit" by Ray Evans and Jay Livingston; "In the Cool, Cool, Cool of the Evening" by Johnny Mercer and Hoagy Carmichael; "Caro Nome" from "Rigoletto" by Verdi. Special Orchestral Arrangements: Van Cleave. Art Directors: Hal Pereira, Earl Hedrick. Set Decorations: Emile Kuri. Editor: Ellsworth Hoagland. Process Photography: Farciot Edouart. Costumes: Edith Head. Assistant Director: Arthur S. Black. Choreography: Charles O'Curran. Special Effects: Gordon Jennings, Paul Lerpae. Associate Producer: Irving Asher. Makeup Supervision: Wally Westmore. Sound: Harry Mills, John Cope.

Cast: Bing Crosby (Pete Garvey), Jane Wyman (Emmadel Jones), Franchot Tone (Wilbur Stanley), Alexis Smith (Winifred Stanley), James Barton (Pa Jones), Connie Gilchrist (Ma Jones), Robert Keith (George Degnan), Jacques Gencel (Robert), Beverly Washburn (Suzi), Walter Catlett (Mr. McGonigle), H. B. Warner (Uncle Elihu), Ian Wolfe (Uncle Adam), Maidel Turner (Aunt Abby), Nicholas Joy (Uncle Prentiss), Anna Maria Alberghetti (Theresa), Alan Reed (Walter Godfrey), Minna Gombell (Mrs. Godfrey); Dorothy Lamour, Louis Armstrong, Phil Harris, Cass Daley, Frank Fontaine (themselves), Irving Bacon (Baines), Chris Appel (Marcel), Charles Halton (Cusick), Charles Lane (Burchard, FBI agent), James Finlayson, Bess Flowers, Frank Hagney, James Burke, Adeline de Walt Reynolds (Aunt Amy), Howard Freeman (governor), Ellen Corby (Mrs. McGonigle), Ted Thorpe (Paul Pippitt), Art Baker (radio announcer), Laura

Elliott (maid), Rev. Neal Dodd (priest), Odette Myrtil (Grey
Lady), Michele Lange (French matron), Charles Sullivan and
Ed Randolph (photographers), Julia Faye, Franklyn Farnum,
Donald Kerr (neighbor), Carl "Alfalfa" Switzer (messenger),
J. Farrell MacDonald, Walter McGrail (newsreel director),
Don Dunning.

An American reporter, Pete Garvey, on assignment
in France at UNESCO headquarters, plans to adopt two
French orphans and then return to the United States to marry
his girl friend, Emmadel Jones. When he arrives with them
in Boston, he finds that she is about to marry a millionaire,
Wilbur Stanley. He makes a deal with Stanley to let him
live in the gate house of the Stanley town house until the
wedding: Pete wants to win Emmadel back; Stanley wants to
make sure it's he she loves. Pete maneuvers Stanley's dis-
tant cousin Winifred toward Stanley while at the same time
he tries to win Emmadel over with the two kids, Robert and
Suzi. At the last minute, during the wedding ceremony, Emmadel decides to marry Pete.

HERE COMES THE GROOM is so completely a Para-
mount/Crosby film, rather than a Frank Capra film, that
the solitary highlight is a special-effect sight gag, like the
Paramountain or the talking fish in ROAD TO UTOPIA or the
talking camels in ROAD TO MOROCCO. All it amounts to
is a clever way of delivering a large chunk of exposition,
but it's a real relief from the plot. In it, Crosby conjures
a live, doll-size replica of Jane Wyman up out of her phono-
graph-record letter, and she tells him her story. (Shades
of FORBIDDEN PLANET and Walter Pidgeon brainstorming
up an image of Anne Francis.) The record sticks, and
Crosby has to kick the table to get the record/Miss Wyman
going again; she falls onto the disc and spins around. You
wait and wait, hoping for a few more like irrelevant bits of
technical ingenuity, knowing that the treacly plot will generate
nothing but itself as it moves from one artificial complication
(Crosby at first plans to adopt only Bobby) to another (he
must marry in five days to keep the kids). You hope for
more effects gags; you fear more assembly-line sophisticated-
sentimental numbers like "Your Own Little House." You get
more numbers.

There are faint echoes of PLATINUM BLONDE and
YOU CAN'T TAKE IT WITH YOU (not to mention IT HAP-
PENED ONE NIGHT and the last-minute switch of wedding

partners), but the similarities in plot seem only coincidental.
There was someone behind those earlier movies; HERE
COMES THE GROOM is a product of departments--music,
costume, writing, special effects--not people.   The script
has no organic strength, but Capra doesn't even take incidental inspiration from it.   There's no imaginative use of
the mansion or lawns or space in general.   The two kids accidentally turn sprinklers on under milling house guests; the
latter get wet.   For this you need Frank Capra?   The unpretentiousness of HERE COMES THE GROOM is only a eu-
phemism for its poverty of invention.   Only very rarely are
you aware of Capra's doing anything but plunking the actors
down before the camera or moving it to keep them before it.

HERE COMES THE GROOM is a sickly, slick combination of sophistication and sentimentality, like the Leo
McCarey LOVE AFFAIR or GOING MY WAY: kids (orphans
yet), music, blindness (Miss Alberghetti), illness (Gencel--
"acute melancholia"), France, and Crosby.   It's difficult to
overcome prejudices against such elements in a movie, especially when the "balancing" comedy is so thin--for instance,
for Miss Alberghetti's solo, when Alan Reed's pantomimic
conducting pretends to offset the pathos of this blind girl,
and the solemnly converging orphans are unmistakably setting
the intended reverential tone.   The comedy isn't the Capra-
McCarey actor-oriented style of the Twenties and Thirties,
but the TV-style situation comedy of McCarey's later RALLY
ROUND THE FLAG, BOYS.   Directors (Capra, McCarey,
Hawks) whose looser, freer Thirties comedies were marvels
of spontaneity and apparent improvisation came studio-pack-
aged with trademarked studio contents in the Fifties.   The
dialogue of HERE COMES THE GROOM, like that of the
Crosby-Hope comedies, is littered with at-the-time-hip ref-
erences to Ma and Pa Kettle, "Annie Get Your Gun," "The
Keys of the Kingdom," etc.   Capra's name is still above the
title, but elsewhere he's not evident, replaced by a studio
formula, derived from other directors, of goo and glibness
and patented studio patter.

There isn't a good, major performance in the movie,
though Robert Keith and others do some good work in the
background.   At first it seems that Alexis Smith is seriously
engaged in the character of dull, boyish Winifred.   When
Pete asks Winifred if anyone ever whistled at her, she replies, offended, "Of course not.   How common," not stooping
for a laugh but truly shocked, which is what's funny.   It's
the difference between an actor's going for a laugh and his

staying in character and letting the laugh come to him.   But
Miss Smith undergoes an embarrassing transformation into a
femme fatale that's obviously going directly for the audience.

Bing Crosby's familiar "effortlessness" wears thin
quickly in HERE COMES THE GROOM.   It matters little if
he usually more or less played himself, but he did it too
often, in the same grooves.   And he perhaps needed a strong
actress opposite him, to start something, like Ingrid Berg-
man in The BELLS OF ST. MARY'S.   His little flourishes
and prestidigitator's motions and his vocal rhythms (in song
and dialogue)--sotto voce asides, abrupt changes of voice,
long speeches suddenly winding down--are overfamiliar.   He's
like a puppet on the script's strings.   You've seen the performance before you've seen the movie.   (In fact, you've
seen the movie before you've seen the movie.)

The script makes Jane Wyman's Emmadel seem dull,
worthless, avaricious, shrill, and, most damning of all, ob-
livious of the dullness and meanness of those around her,
such as Franchot Tone's small-minded millionaire, who be-
littles Emmadel's drab past and her crudely utilitarian future
as his wife.   (She is to give the Stanley family babies in exchange for luxury.)   Miss Wyman shrinks to fit every demand: child-producer for Tone, wife for Crosby, mother
for the tots.   She actually reacts with delight when she's
told that she's to produce "colts."[1]   The script, at various
times, has her say things like, "I was born to be a mother"
and "I'm going to have to be such a good wife to deserve all
of this."   The flesh fairly creeps.   Her role seems designed
to make marriage for a woman seem truly repugnant.   Miss
Wyman is the perfect situation comedienne, blind to the uglier
implications of her part, noisy, intent on making her character more childishly petulant than necessary in an effort to
make her amusing.

Tone seems less affected by the exigencies of the
script.   His first scene, in which Stanley and Garvey com-
pare talents and accomplishments, is both his and Crosby's
best.   They're obviously vying as actors as well as characters, and the competition brings out the best in them.   But
Tone has little to do after that but look superior and sophisticated.

James Barton, as Miss Wyman's socially embarrassing
father, all but capsizes doing the animated-old-reprobate bit.
Beverly Washburn has a winning gap-toothed smile, but she

and Jacques Gencel as the orphans are too obviously calculated as little heart-tuggers.   Capra standby Charles Lane,
as a reporter who impersonates an FBI agent and unites
Crosby, Wyman, and the children, has a nice exit line ("Don't
I get a byline?").   (Lane, H. B. Warner, Walter Catlett, and
Irving Bacon are the only happy associations with past Capra's.)   But all anyone has at best is a moment or a line.

Note

1.   There's a comic inconsistency between the script's avoid-
     ance of innocuous three- and four-letter words and the
     use of stronger words like "barren" to describe Wini-
     fred and "produce" to describe the Stanleys.   Degnan
     calls long distance and orders Garvey, "Get your ...
     get yourself back here."   Emmadel demurely catches
     herself at one point, "I'm going to learn to be a lady
     come ... well, come high water."   But the comedy
     is unintentional.

PART IV

HARRY LANGDON

Chapter 16

The STRONG MAN

First National/Harry Langdon Corp. 1926. 75 minutes
(7 reels).

Director: Frank Capra. Screenplay: Arthur Ripley, Frank
Capra, Hal Conklin, Robert Eddy. Comedy Construction:
Clarence Hennecke. Photography: Elgin Lessley, Glenn
Kershner. Editor: Harold Young. One of the ten greatest
films--Claude Autant-Lara, Brussels poll of directors, 1952.

        Cast: Harry Langdon (Paul Bergot), Gertrude Astor
(Gold Tooth), Priscilla Bonner (Mary Brown), William V.
Mong (Parson Brown), Arthur Thalasso (Zandow the Great),
Robert McKim (Roy McDevitt), Brooks Benedict (bus passen-
ger), Tay Garnett?

        During World War I, Mary Brown, an American girl,
writes letters to a Belgian soldier, Paul Bergot, on the German front. He loses track of her when he is taken prisoner
by the enemy. After the Armistice he comes to America as
part of the act of weight-lifter Zandow the Great, the German who captured him.

        Paul begins his search for Mary by standing on a
street corner watching the passersby, hoping to recognize
her from a photo she sent him. A thief's moll, trying to
shake a detective, stashes a wad of bills in Paul's pocket.
She then tries to retrieve it without letting him know that he
has it. But the bills slip through a hole into the lining of
his coat. She tries to inveigle him into coming up to her
apartment by posing as Mary. But her manner (uncouth--
she manages to smoke cigarettes crudely even with a hold-
er), size (large), and appearance (not too similar to the picture of Mary) make him reluctant to join her. She feigns
fainting, and a hotel doorman insists that Paul carry her to

her room. ("You can't leave your women lying around like
that.") He has difficulty carrying her up the hotel stairs to
her room and when he finally makes it she thanks him by
attacking him with an ice pick. She retrieves the money,
and Paul leaves surreptitiously. ("Don't let this leak out.")
He rejoins Zandow.

Paul finally finds Mary, the blind daughter of a minister, in the small town of Cloverdale, which Zandow's act is
playing. Cloverdale is overrun with bootleggers and other
bad elements. When Zandow is found drunk before he is
scheduled to go on at the local music hall, Paul is forced to
take his place. Thanks to him, a brawl breaks out, and,
with the aid of a cannon, he runs the rabble out of town.

If Harry Langdon's work, apparently represented at
its best by his two Capra-directed movies, The STRONG
MAN and LONG PANTS, at first seems disappointing, the
disappointment is not so very different from the disappointment one may feel at seeing the body of films of any of the
classic comedians of the Twenties and Thirties and finding
so few of them to be as "great" as they're all supposed to
be. True, those classic silents and early talkies of Keaton,
Chaplin, Fields, and the Marx Brothers are almost all to
some degree good, but only the Marxes' Paramounts could,
I think, as a group, be called great. In Langdon's case
one's sense of disappointment is exaggerated since he made
so few films and perhaps no truly great ones. Fine as The
STRONG MAN is--and it's by far the best Langdon I've seen
--it falls just short of greatness. Perhaps if he had stayed
on with Capra he would have gone on to make some great
comedies. The STRONG MAN is half--the first half--of a
great comedy.

Much of the time Langdon's--and Buster Keaton's,
Harold Lloyd's, and even Charlie Chaplin's--"characters"
(and this doesn't diminish their accomplishments) were simply pegs for gags, disappointingly when the gags weren't that
inspired, joyously when they were inspired (see The KID
BROTHER, SEVEN CHANCES, SHERLOCK JUNIOR). Only
in retrospect can enough data and biographical detail be culled
from their movies even to begin to support fine theories of
character. Film for film there just isn't that much "to" the
Keaton or Chaplin screen personality. Their personae can
be summed up in a few sentences. They built on their personae, but what they built (and it wasn't character studies)
was far more important and substantial than that on which

they built.

In The STRONG MAN, Harry Langdon's child-like persona is one of revulsion at displays of violence and other adult pastimes such as sex and crime, and an idiot persistence at provoking acts of violence, primarily against himself. (He keeps taking pokes at people even though he always gets punched back much more convincingly.) A more productive way of defining and discussing silent comedy than in terms of characterization is in terms of prop-oriented and actor-oriented comedy. The former relies on stunts with objects (in The STRONG MAN, Langdon's unrolling of the music-hall-stage curtain over the crowd) or mechanical wonders; the latter, on the movements and expressions of actors, or pantomime.

The best sections of The STRONG MAN are built almost wholly on Langdon's eccentric movements: a sidling shuffle, a half-punch, a half-turn, a sidelong dirty look; a hand kiss stolen, absurdly, from under the eyes of a blind girl--the furtive, hesitant gestures of one who half-does things. Often no props are necessary, only Langdon and another person. Capra's thumbnail description of Langdon probably cannot be improved upon: "You could practically see the wheels of his immature mind turning as it registered tiny pleasures or discomforts. Langdon himself was a virtuoso of flitting, hesitant motions. In the middle of extreme danger he could be distracted by a butterfly, or a spot of dirt on his finger."[1]

The brightest example of this pantomimic comedy of indecision is Paul's encounter with Gold Tooth, an extended sequence which, amazingly, builds a series of interlocking comic routines--Paul following Gold Tooth; the woman fainting, with Paul uncertain as to what to do with the body, etc. --on a wisp of a basis: her attempts to retrieve the wad of bills from his coat. It's a sequence which, excerpted from the movie, would constitute a great short. It's a testament to the writer and director who can recognize a good thing when they see it, and to hell with the plot; a testament to the art of making something out of nothing. Later in the sequence, props--a ladder, a vase--are introduced. But most of it consists of Langdon's balletic gyrations around an active or--like a prop--inert Gold Tooth.

The STRONG MAN is flawed not by an episodic structure, but by an inability to assimilate plot elements. The

fault lies not so much in haphazard plotting as in the fact
that the movie feels it must answer to the demands of the
plot.   The revelation of Mary Brown as a blind girl and the
establishment of her father as a parson fighting town corruption rightly lead one to expect a big payoff.   But you soon
find out that what you're watching is not so much a laborious
set-up as a laborious explanation.   Mary is blind not because her blindness will figure in the plot, except tangential-
ly, but because it accounts for her "disappearance," which in
turn accounted for Paul's wanderings, which was the main
idea.   It's as if the script were written around that one idea
and the writers felt that it was so good that it justified any
amount of explaining.   Mary is an anti-climax, and the best
one can say for her is that she doesn't regain her sight.
(Mute or blind characters are usually written into movies
only so that they can be cured near the end.)

Parson Brown's presence makes possible a rather
tired Biblical framework for the Cloverdale scenes, in which
Cloverdale is Jericho; Paul, Joshua; and the apocalyptic cannon, the trumpet that makes good the Joshua conceit.[2]   And
Paul's triumph over the parson's foes gives him an "in" with
his daughter.

The parson and his daughter remain, to the end, servants of the plot since both are, unfortunately, untappable
for low-comic purposes, representing as they do religion and
physical handicap, respectively, which means that they must
be treated with reverence and--that bane of comedy--respect
(somewhat as the condemned man, Earl Williams, is treated
at first in HIS GIRL FRIDAY).   Their scenes must be tip-
toed through, treated delicately and with "taste": or, how
to get nothing out of something.   In theory, Mary is the
heart of the movie; in fact, the gun moll is.

In some notes on Chaplin's CITY LIGHTS,[3] Stanley
Kauffmann proposes a hierarchy of silent comedians, with
Chaplin and Keaton at the top, Lloyd below them, and Langdon at the bottom.   It's only a note, based on only a few
titles, but even as a note it's defective in that it ranks its
subjects according to emotional effectiveness, which gauge
applies fairly frequently to Chaplin, infrequently to Langdon,
Keaton, and Lloyd.   And it calls The STRONG MAN "a coy
bore, begging pitifully for pathos."   This is a wild misrep-
resentation of the movie, a judgment of the whole by a part
--Mary Brown's scenes--in fact by a part that's not even
assimilated into the whole; in actuality, it's a misrepresenta-

tion of that part.

The problem with the Mary Brown sequence is not that it "begs." It's just that it's treated as a necessary evil. It serves no other purpose than to justify sequences in retrospect. It leads nowhere. And it's certainly not "pitiful," though it might as well be--it's tasteful. It's done with the kind of tastefulness that leaves one yearning for a little tastelessness.

One wishes that Capra and company had either treated the Cloverdale end of the plot as offhandedly as Langdon's capture by the German--the hulk finds Langdon sitting mooning against a tree and simply drags him off[4]--or that they had simply junked the Cloverdale section. In its place they could have developed Langdon's odyssey further. (As it is, it's rather a short odyssey.)

Notes

1.   The Name above the Title, p. 62.

2.   The use of the cannon to end Langdon's strong-man act is a good example of an unassimilated plot element. It completes the conceit, but doesn't evolve naturally out of the sequence.

3.   Film Comment, September-October, 1972, p. 19.

4.   The height of economy, that feat also anticipates the weight-lifting act.

Chapter 17

OTHER LANGDONS

LONG PANTS. First National/Harry Langdon Corp. 1927.
60 minutes (6 reels).

Director: Frank Capra. Story: Arthur Ripley. Adaptation: Robert Eddy. Photography: Elgin Lessley, Glenn
Kershner. Comedy Construction: Clarence Hennecke.

 Cast: Harry Langdon (The Boy), Alma Bennett (The
Vamp, Bebe Blair), Priscilla Bonner (Priscilla), Gladys
Brockwell (the mother), Al Roscoe (the father), Frankie
Darro (Harry as a small boy), Betty Francisco.

 The Boy, who sees himself in daydreams as a Don
Juan, convinces his mother to let him wear long pants. He
bicycles down the street to show himself off to the neighbors and meets and falls for a city vamp. He rides around
her car, trying to impress her with bicycle tricks. His
parents want him to marry the girl next door, but, true to
his new-found love, he decides that he must do away with
the girl. He takes her into the woods and tries to shoot
her. But he is obliged, when he gets caught in a bear trap,
to abandon the idea. When he later learns that the vamp
has been arrested (for smuggling "snow"), he goes to her
rescue and is himself jailed. After learning that the vamp
killed her husband, he decides to return to the girl.

 LONG PANTS divides neatly--rather too neatly--into
three or four good comedy routines and other, lesser,
bridging sequences. It's one of the most mechanical of silent comedies, yet it's mechanically effective. The bicycle
sequence is especially-well-developed. But The STRONG
MAN is the Langdon comedy.

LUCKY STARS. Pathe/Sennett. 1925. 20 minutes (2 reels).

Director: Harry Edwards. Screenplay: Frank Capra,
Arthur Ripley. Photography: George Crocker. Editor:
William Hornbeck.

Cast: Harry Langdon, Vernon Dent.

The top-hatted Langdon and Dent are a potentially fine
con-man team, but this short meanders more than most silent-comedy features. When nothing much develops in one
place, it moves on to another. Noteworthy gag: Langdon
staring vacantly at the now-useless key to his smashed ward-
robe trunk, then gingerly tossing it on the ground near the
trunk. Noteworthy ballet sequence: Langdon dancing around
a tantalizing, forbidden glass of beer in the middle of a street
and all but diving into it before reluctantly moving on.

PLAIN CLOTHES. Pathe/Sennett. 1925. 2 reels.

Director: Harry Edwards. Screenplay: Frank Capra,
Arthur Ripley.

Cast: Harry Langdon, Claire Cushman, Jean Hath-
away, Vernon Dent, William McCall.

SATURDAY AFTERNOON. Pathe/Sennett. 1926. 30
minutes (3 reels).

Director: Harry Edwards. Screenplay: Frank Capra,
Arthur Ripley. Titles: A. H. Giebler.

Cast: Harry Langdon, Alice Ward, Vernon Dent,
Ruth Hiatt, Peggy Montgomery.

Edwards over-emphasizes and over-exposes the Langdon trademarks. (Langdon goes through his "indecisive" act
at length twice.) Even the better gags (Harry surreptitiously
"pushing" a kiss at a girl) are so drawn out that they become self-conscious.

TRAMP, TRAMP, TRAMP. First National/Harry Langdon
Corp. 1926. 62 minutes (6 reels).

Director: Harry Edwards; (uncredited) Frank Capra. Story:
Capra, Tim Whelan, Hal Conklin, J. Frank Holliday, Gerald
Duffy, Murray Roth. Photography: Elgin Lessley (and
George Spear?).

     Cast: Harry Langdon (Harry), Joan Crawford (Betty
Burton), Edwards Davis (John Burton), Carlton Griffin (Roger
Caldwell), Alec B. Francis (Harry's father), Brooks Bene-
dict (taxi driver), Tom Murray (the Argentine).

     Although TRAMP, TRAMP, TRAMP is pretty good
comedy, it stirs up my latent resentment of silent movies.
It's probably natural for those who grew up on silents to
think of talkies as hampered by sound and for those who
grew up on talkies to think of silents as hampered by silence.
Silent-people can, if they wish, take it as testimony to the
superior art of their form that talkie-people have to watch
silents more closely to appreciate them--art implying the
spectator's active involvement--but we talkie-people can interpret this strain to mean that silents are simply hard to
watch. With little aural stimulus (organ or piano accom-
paniment helps some), the mind is left to wander even as
the eyes are focused on the silent movie on the screen. I
often find that I have to force myself to concentrate on a
silent, even a good one. And comedians like Harry Langdon
and Laurel and Hardy, who built whole scenes on twitches
and smirks and the minutest movements, demand the utmost
concentration. (Laurel and Hardy comedies without a strong
central gimmick I find almost unwatchable.) And at times,
with Langdon, the line between pantomime and plain mugging
begins to disappear as the camera takes root before him and
watches as, like a malfunctioning mechanical man, he sput-
ters on and on and almost defies you to stop watching his
every little spasm.

     Unlike The STRONG MAN, TRAMP, TRAMP, TRAMP
sometimes stagnates when it dwells on Langdon's balletic
flutterings. Instead of developing his actions and reactions
into routines, the writers and director set up situations and
let Langdon flail through them until he runs down. His flail-
ings are usually amusing, but their duration seems arbitrary,
decided by how many variations on a gag the writers happened to come up with. (With six writers, it's not surprising that they came up with so many.) TRAMP, TRAMP,
TRAMP is amusing, but it doesn't build, either within sequences or from sequence to sequence. There's no back-
bone, so it's all up to Langdon's starts and stops in Joan

Crawford's presence.

HIS FIRST FLAME.   Pathe/Mack Sennett Special.   1926
(released 1927).   70 minutes (6 reels).

Director: Harry Edwards.   Screenplay: Arthur Ripley,
Frank Capra.   Photography: William Williams, Ernie
Crockett.

        Cast: Harry Langdon (Harry Howells), Ruth Hiatt
(Mary Morgan), Natalie Kingston (Ethel Morgan), Vernon
Dent (Amos McCarthy), Bud Jamison (Hector Benedict), Dot
Farley (Mrs. Benedict).

        (Comments based on a three-reel version.)

        Harry starts off with flowers and a present for his
girl, but is detained by shoplifters, his uncle, and a fire.
There are no real, developed routines, but there is an
hilarious string of gags with the flowers and gift.   Harry's
uncle disapproves of his engagement and, when he catches
him with the flowers, Harry panics and pretends they're
for his uncle.   The latter summarily tosses them ("the
flowers of love") into a spittoon.   Later, Harry crushes a
new bouquet getting into a cab and is left with the stems.
Intending to throw them out, he tosses out the present and
is again left with stems.   He tries to retrieve the package,
and a truck runs over it.   The comic disparity between this
mild little man's humble intentions and the disasters that be-
fall him lends the early scenes some coherence.   Then the
movie begins to wander.   There is one great gag in which
Harry thinks he has walked out of a store with a woman's
leg.   He carefully lays this dummy leg down ("Oh, my God,
I didn't want your leg!" his face says as clearly as a title)
and, burdened with guilt for his terrible act, runs off.

        In HIS FIRST FLAME, Langdon has a general idea of
how things work, but no specific ideas.   He knows he can
talk into a phone but not that he might as well stop talking
into it after he hangs up.   And when he thinks, his hands
and legs flutter and dance about, uncontrolled.

APPENDICES

Appendix I

OTHER FILMS DIRECTED BY FRANK CAPRA

The BALLAD OF FISHER'S BOARDING HOUSE. Pathe.
1922. 12 minutes (1 reel). (aka BALLAD OF FULTAH
FISHER'S BOARDING HOUSE).

Director: Frank Capra. Based on the poem, "Ballad of
Fisher's Boarding-House" (in Departmental Ditties and Other
Verses), by Rudyard Kipling. Photography: Roy Wiggins.
Producer: Walter Montague.

 A girl, "Anne of Austria," precipitates a bloody brawl
in a sailor's boarding house. One sailor, Hans, is killed.
Searching his body, Anne comes across a silver crucifix and
places it next to her heart. Thus she "rises from the depths
of degradation...."

> ... stirring at all times and unusually rich in
> characterization ... a masterpiece of realism,
> carrying dramatic value and a spiritual flavor.--
> Laurence Reid, Motion Picture News, April 15,
> 1922, p. 2216.

FOR THE LOVE OF MIKE. First National/Robert Kane.
1927. 75 minutes (7 reels). (aka LOVE O'MIKE).

Director: Frank Capra. Screenplay: J. Clarkson Miller.
Photography: Ernest Haller. Based on the story, "Hell's
Kitchen," by John Moroso.

 Cast: Claudette Colbert (Mary), Ben Lyon (Mike),
George Sidney (Abraham Katz), Ford Sterling (Herman
Schultz), Hugh Cameron (Patrick O'Malley), Richard "Skeets"
Gallagher (Coxey Pendleton), Rudolph Cameron (Henry Sharp),
Mabel Swor (Evelyn Joyce).

As a baby, Mike is abandoned on the doorstep of a
tenement in Hell's Kitchen. He is reared by Herman Schultz,
Abie Katz, and Patrick O'Malley, who support him through
high school.   Mary, a pretty Italian cashier in Schultz's deli-
catessen, persuades Mike to enter Yale, where he distinguishes himself socially and athletically. He becomes involved with a crooked gambler who threatens to have him
arrested unless he throws a race. But Mike rows the Yale
team to victory and, in the process, wins Mary's heart.

> ... just seven reels of mediocre film. --Frank
> Capra, The Name above the Title, p. 76.

THAT CERTAIN THING. Columbia. 1928. 69 minutes (7
reels).

Director: Frank Capra. Screenplay: Elmer Harris. Titles:
Al Boasberg. Photography: Joseph Walker. Art Director:
Robert E. Lee. Editor: Arthur Roberts. Assistant Direc-
tor: Eugene De Rue.

Cast: Viola Dana (Molly Kelly), Ralph Graves (Andy
B. Charles, Jr.), Burr McIntosh (A. B. Charles, Sr.),
Aggie Herring (Mrs. Maggie Kelly), Carl Gerard (Brooks),
Syd Crossley (valet).

Molly Kelly, a cigarstand drudge, marries Andy B.
Charles, Jr., idle son of wealthy A. B. Charles, a res-
taurateur. Mr. Charles disinherits his son when he hears
of the marriage, forcing him to work as a day laborer.
Eating a box lunch prepared by Molly gives Andy an inspiration to open an eatery--the "Molly Box Lunch Company."
When Andy's father, the owner of a nearby restaurant whose
business is falling off, visits the entrepreneurs, he is so
pleased to find that his son is a success that he gives the
couple money to expand their business.

> Here is an indie that gives A-1 entertainment ...
> a strong, laugh-comedy romance materially aided
> by Boasberg's titles.... Directing is splendid....
> --Mark., Variety, May 2, 1928.

> ... budgeted at less than twenty thousand dol-
> lars.... We even saved lunch money on location
> by eating our own props--the box lunches. --Frank
> Capra, The Name above the Title, p. 84.

SO THIS IS LOVE. Columbia. 1928. 60 minutes (6 reels).

Director: Frank Capra. Continuity: Rex Taylor. Adaptation: Elmer Harris. Story: Norman Springer. Photography: Ray June. Art Director: Robert E. Lee. Editor: Arthur Roberts. Producer: Harry Cohn. Assistant Director: Eugene De Rue.

Cast: Shirley Mason (Hilda Jensen), William Collier, Jr. (Jerry McGuire), Johnnie Walker (Spike Mullins), Ernie Adams (Flash Tracy), Carl Gerard (Otto), William H. Strauss (Maison Katz), Jean Laverty (Mary Malone).

Jerry McGuire, a dress designer, and Spike Mullins, a boxer, vie for the attentions of counter girl Hilda Jensen. At a dance, Spike takes her away from Jerry and tosses him out on his ear. Jerry takes boxing lessons and, when he wins a match, he wins Hilda too.

> Some of the funniest work is accomplished by Shirley Mason when she feeds the champ on everything she has in the store before he meets her boy friend. --Variety, May 2, 1928.

> ... impossible yarn.... Direction ... not good. --Film Daily, April 22, 1928, p. 8.

> Better than the run of Columbia pictures; has some ferocious ring fighting and some good comedy.-- Roy W. Adams, theatre owner, Exhibitors Herald, December 22, 1928, p. 51.

The MATINEE IDOL. Columbia. 1928. 66 minutes (6 reels).

Director: Frank R. Capra. Continuity: Peter Milne. Adaptation: Elmer Harris. From Robert Lord and Ernest Pagano's "Come Back to Aaron." Photography: Phillip Tannura. Art Director: Robert E. Lee. Editor: Arthur Roberts. Assistant Director: Eugene De Rue. Producer: Harry Cohn.

Cast: Bessie Love (Ginger Bolivar), Johnnie Walker (Don Wilson/Harry Mann), Lionel Belmore (Col. Jaspar Bolivar), Ernest Hilliard (Wingate), Sidney D'Albrook (J. Madison Wilberforce), David Mir (Eric Barrymaine).

To pass the time, members of a vacationing New York theater company attend the Great Bolivar Stock Company's Civil War melodrama. Don Wilson, of the New York company, is accidentally hired to play a part in the show by Ginger Bolivar, star of the production and daughter of the producer. Don's friends are so convulsed over the performance that they make arrangements to bring the group to New York. There Ginger discovers how they have been duped and, thinking she has failed as a dramatic actress, returns home. A few days later, Don arrives to declare his love for her.

> Solid laugh and hoke picture.... Capra, directing, passes up chances to emphasize the pathos when the girl and her father realize their performance is being laughed at.... A traveling camera to a closeup ... might have brought a lump to many a throat, but the film is too concerned with laughs. All of which it gets.... --Sid., Variety, April 25, 1928.

> Looks as if Frank Capra has proved he doesn't need a Harry Langdon to prove he's a comedy director. He ... builds [the story] into a succession of howls and giggles. Direction ... aces. -- Film Daily, April 29, 1928.

> An excellent entertaining picture from every angle. Acting exceptionally good. Comedy clean and thoroughly amusing. --theatre owner, Exhibitors Herald, November 3, 1928, p. 69.

> One of the best Columbia has ever made. --theatre owner, Exhibitors Herald, November 3, 1928, p. 69.

The WAY OF THE STRONG. Columbia. 1928. 61 minutes (6 reels).

Director: Frank Capra. Screenplay: Peter Milne. Story: William Conselman. Photography: Ben Reynolds. Producer: Harry Cohn.

Cast: Mitchell Lewis (Handsome Williams), Alice Day (Nora), Margaret Livingston (Marie), Theodore von Eltz (Dan), William Norton Bailey (Tiger Louie).

Handsome Williams, king of the bootleggers, falls in love with Nora, a beautiful blind violinist, and gives her a job in his cafe. Handsome (who's actually ugly) convinces the girl that he is handsome, and she begins to return his affection. Tiger Louie, a bootlegger out to get Handsome, kidnaps Nora and forces Handsome to give his trucks free entry into the city. Handsome leads a raid on Louie's place and, with the help of Dan, the piano player, rescues Nora. Running from the police, Handsome realizes that Dan and Nora are in love. He sacrifices his life to give them time to get to safety.

> I was too inexperienced to handle the delicate nuances or the sustained moods of dramatic conflict. --Frank Capra, The Name above the Title, p. 86.

> Fair entertainment. Better than cheap Westerns at the box office, but nothing to rave over, at that. --L. E. Palmer, theatre owner, Exhibitors Herald, January 12, 1929, p. 67.

> Good underworld drama ... a picture with real thrills, love, interest, suspense--everything.... Direction ... fine. --Film Daily, August 12, 1928.

> Personally did not think this anything but ordinary. --Marion F. Bodwell, theatre owner, Exhibitors Herald, December 1, 1928, p. 67.

SAY IT WITH SABLES. Columbia. 1928. 70 minutes (7 reels).

Director: Frank Capra. Screenplay: Dorothy Howell. Story: Frank Capra, Peter Milne. Photography: Joseph Walker. Art Director: Harrison Wiley. Editor: Arthur Roberts. Producer: Harry Cohn. Assistant Director: Joe Nadel.

Cast: Francis X. Bushman (John Caswell), Helene Chadwick (Helen Caswell), Margaret Livingston (Irene Gordon), Arthur Rankin (Doug Caswell), June Nash (Marie Caswell), Alphonz Ethier (Mitchell), Edna Mae Cooper (maid).

John Caswell, a wealthy widower, breaks with gold-digger Irene Gordon, his mistress, and takes Helen for his

wife. Later, his son, Doug, returns from college with his
fiancée, who turns out to be Irene. Caswell tells Doug that
Irene was his mistress, and Doug, unbelieving, goes to
Irene's apartment to confront her. John follows him. He
finds Irene dead of a gunshot wound and arranges the apartment so that her death appears to be a suicide. The following morning, homicide detective Mitchell comes to the Caswell home, and John confesses to the murder. Mitchell,
however, finds the mate of an earring he picked up at the
scene of the crime among Helen's things. He accuses her
of Irene's murder. Helen tells him that the shooting was
accidental, and Mitchell officially closes the case, ruling the
death a suicide.

> ... well done ... pretty slow in developing. --
> Film Daily, August 12, 1928.

> Very, very good. Margaret Livingston has the
> best part she ever had, in this town anyway. --
> Frank Johnson, theatre owner, Exhibitors Herald,
> December 8, 1928, p. 67.

> ... my experiment with drama was dismal. --
> Frank Capra, The Name above the Title, p. 86.

SUBMARINE.   Columbia.   1928.   93 minutes (9 reels).

Director: Frank R. Capra; begun by Irvin Willat. Screenplay: Dorothy Howell. Story: Norman Springer. Photography: Joseph Walker. Art Director: Harrison Wiley. Editor: Arthur Roberts. Producer: Harry Cohn. Assistant
Director: Buddy Coleman. Song: "Pals, Just Pals," by
Herman Ruby and Dave Dreyer.

Cast: Jack Holt (Jack Dorgan), Dorothy Revier (Bessie), Ralph Graves (Bob Mason), Clarence Burton (submarine
commander), Arthur Rankin (the boy).

Jack Dorgan, a warrant officer and an expert deep-
sea diver, marries Bessie, a dancehall girl. Shortly thereafter, he is ordered out into the Pacific to work on a wreck.
Meanwhile, Bob Mason, a fellow officer and Jack's best
friend, meets Bessie at the Oakland dancehall. Bessie
doesn't tell Bob that she is married. Jack returns to port
and, discovering them in each other's arms, accuses Bob
of forcing himself on Bessie. Bob's submarine later sinks,

and the crew is trapped inside. Jack, the only diver in the
fleet good enough to reach the men, is too dispirited to care.
Bessie at last confesses that she and not Bob was to blame
for the affair, and Jack rescues the trapped men.

> SUBMARINE ... is one of the most exciting films
> I have seen.... There is a certain strength about
> this film, due not so much to the acting of any in-
> dividual ... or to the plot, as to the practical and
> essential part which aeroplanes, submarines and
> diving contraptions play in the story. --Celia Simp-
> son, The Spectator, May 18, 1929, p. 776.

The POWER OF THE PRESS. Columbia. 1928. 62 minutes
(7 reels).

Director: Frank Capra. Screenplay: Frederick Thompson,
Sonya Levien. Photography: Chet Lyons, Ted Tetzlaff.
Art Director: Harrison Wiley. Editor: Frank Atkinson.
Producer: Jack Cohn. Assistant Director: Buddy Coleman.

Cast: Douglas Fairbanks, Jr. (Clem Rogers),
Jobyna Ralston (Jane Atwill), Mildred Harris (Marie), Philo
McCullough (Blake), Wheeler Oakman (Van), Robert Edeson
(city editor), Edwards Davis (Mr. Atwill), Del Henderson
(Johnson), Charles Clary (district attorney).

The district attorney is murdered. Clem Rogers, a
cub reporter, discovers that Jane Atwill, the daughter of a
mayoral candidate, was present when the crime was com-
mitted. The story makes page one, and Jane is arrested.
She insists that she has no idea who fired the fatal shot and
is released on bail; but her father's political chances are
ruined. She angrily goes to the paper and convinces Clem
of her innocence. Working together, Clem and Jane eventually prove that Blake, her father's political opponent, was
responsible for the murder. Clem again has a front page
story, and he and Jane are married.

> Of the remaining six silent films which [Capra]
> directed in the same year and early 1929, The
> POWER OF THE PRESS is probably the best....
> The film is fast and efficient ... and the playing
> has a delightful feeling for light comedy. --David
> Robinson, Hollywood in the Twenties, 1970, p. 138.

Exciting and ... engaging melodrama with a light
touch that lifts it out of the stencil class.... Capra's directorial job above average.... Young Fairbanks improves rapidly as a light comedian. --
Land., <u>Variety,</u> December 5, 1928.

Ordinary program fare.... Nothing new in all
this, but it is handled with a certain directorial
sprightliness that makes it seem reasonably fresh.
--<u>Film Daily,</u> December 2, 1928.

About as good a little program attraction as we've
shown this year ... strong suspense through the
entire picture.--**W.** H. Hedberg, theatre owner,
<u>Exhibitors Herald,</u> March 16, 1929, p. 63.

The YOUNGER GENERATION. Columbia. 1929. 75 minutes.
silent & talking-sequence versions.

Director: Frank R. Capra. Screenplay: Sonya Levien.
Based on Fannie Hurst's play, "It is To Laugh." Dialogue:
Howard J. Green. Photography: Teddy Tetzlaff. Art Di-
rector: Harrison Wiley. Technical Director: Edward
Shulter. Editor: Arthur Roberts. Producer: Jack Cohn.
Assistant Director: Tenny Wright. Production Manager:
Joe Cook.

        Cast: Jean Hersholt (Julius Goldfish), Lina Basquette
(Birdie Goldfish), Rosa Rosanova (Tildie Goldfish), Ricardo
Cortez (Morris), Rex Lease (Eddie Lesser), Martha Frank-
lin (Mrs. Lesser), Julia Swayne Gordon (Mrs. Striker),
Julanne Johnston (Irma Striker), Jack Raymond (Pinsky), Syd
Crossley (butler), Otto Fries (tradesman).

        Morris Goldfish, the son of a Jewish immigrant family
living on New York's lower East Side, becomes a successful
Fifth Avenue antique dealer.   He changes his name to Fish
and moves his parents and sister, Birdie, into his plush
Park Avenue apartment.   Birdie is in love with Eddie, a
struggling song writer; Morris, trying to improve his family's position, wants to marry the daughter of the wealthy
Kahns.   Birdie marries Eddie, and, when Eddie is arrested
for his part in a jewel robbery, Morris orders her out of
his apartment.   Pa Goldfish leaves after being called a servant before the Kahns.   He dies happily after a family recon-
ciliation.

Sentimental oil has been spread on thick and often
spills over.... The film has a particularly morbid finish ... the old man dies--probably the most
literal and graphic decease ever screened in a
light dramatic release.--Rush., Variety, March 20,
1929.

The film is not typical Capra, but it does reflect
his prowess in developing and animating a narra-
tive--in this case a pretty maudlin one ... awkward.....--Tom Shales, in The American Film
Heritage, 1972, p. 118.

The DONOVAN AFFAIR. Columbia. 1929. 83 minutes.
sound & silent versions.

Director: Frank R. Capra. Screenplay: Dorothy Howell.
Dialogue, Titles: Howard J. Green. From the play by
Owen Davis. Photography: Teddy Tetzlaff. Art Director:
Harrison Wiley. Editor: Arthur Roberts. Producer: Har-
ry Cohn. Assistant Director: Tenny Wright.

Cast: Jack Holt (Inspector Killian), Dorothy Revier
(Jean Rankin), William Collier, Jr. (Cornish), Agnes Ayres
(Lydia Rankin), John Roche (Jack Donovan), Fred Kelsey
(Carney), Hank Mann (Dr. Lindsey), Wheeler Oakman (Por-
ter), Virginia Browne Faire (Mary Mills), Alphonse Ethier
(Capt. Peter Rankin), Edward Hearn (Nelson), Ethel Wales
(Mrs. Lindsey), John Wallace (Dobbs).

(A caption at the beginning of the picture requests
those in the audience not to reveal the identity of the killer.)

The lights in the room where a dinner party is being
held are turned off so that all may observe the effect of a
cat's-eye ring worn by gambler-philanderer Jack Donovan.
While the lights are out, Donovan is stabbed to death with a
carving knife. Inspector Killian at first suspects Porter, a
criminal present at the killing who was on bad terms with
Donovan. He recreates the circumstances of the crime at
Peter Rankin's home. (Rankin's wife was being blackmailed
by Donovan.) Just as Porter is about to tell Killian who he
suspects is the murderer, Porter is himself murdered.
Killian finally discovers that Nelson, the butler, who was
angry with Donovan for playing around with Mary Mills, a
servant, is the killer.

> Columbia has a strong dialog feature here that can
> stand the de luxe test anywhere. In addition to a
> well-conceived and neatly developed cock robin yarn
> there are laughs liberally sprinkled along the way,
> obtained through by-play with a minimum of mug-
> ging. --Land., Variety, May 1, 1929.

> Making The DONOVAN AFFAIR, I believe, was the
> beginning of a true understanding of the skills of
> my craft: how to make the mechanics--lighting,
> microphone, camera--serve and be subject to the
> actors.....--Frank Capra, The Name above the
> Title, p. 105.

FLIGHT.   Columbia. 1929. 110 minutes. sound & silent
versions.

Director: Frank R. Capra. Screenplay: Howard J. Green.
Dialogue: Capra. Story: Ralph Graves. Photography:
Joseph Walker, Joe Novak. Assistants: Elmer Dyer, Paul
Perry. Art Director: Harrison Wiley. Editors: Ben Pivar,
Maurice Wright, Gene Milford. Sound Engineers: John Liva-
dary, Harry Blanchard, Eddie Hahn, Ellis Gray. Assistant
Director: Buddy Coleman.

Cast: Jack Holt (Panama Williams), Lila Lee (Elinor),
Ralph Graves (Lefty Phelps), Alan Roscoe (Major), Harold
Goodwin (Steve Roberts), Jimmy De La Cruze (Lobo/Sandino).

After running the wrong way with the football at a
crucial point in a Harvard-Yale game, Lefty Phelps joins the
flying squad of the Marines. Williams, who was present at
the game, sympathizes with the boy and becomes his pal.
Lefty falls in love with Elinor, a nurse. When he later discovers that she is Williams' girl, he treats her with indifference. The two men leave for Nicaragua to assist in quell-
ing a revolutionary uprising. Williams asks Lefty to propose
to Elinor for him. He does so, but she confesses that she
loves him and not Williams. When Lefty is lost in the jun-
gle, Williams flies to his rescue and is injured. Lefty flies
him to the landing base and, with the approval of his pal, is
united with Elinor.

> Capra's guts show in a cremation scene. It's
> probably the first cremation bit ever put on the
> screen or stage ... but it's not gruesome, the

way it is done..... --Sime, <u>Variety,</u> September 18, 1929.

During those all too brief moments when the producer skips away from melodramatic flubdub, tedious romantic passages and slapstick comedy and turns to scenes of airplanes in formation and flying stunts, FLIGHT ... is well worth watching. --Mordaunt Hall, The New York <u>Times,</u> September 14, 1929, p. 17.

... exciting, jingoistic..... --Elliott Stein, <u>Sight and Sound</u>, Summer 1972, p. 164.

LADIES OF LEISURE. Columbia. 1930. 98 minutes. sound & silent versions.

Director: Frank Capra. Screenplay: Jo Swerling. Titles: Dudley Early. Based on the play, "Ladies of the Evening," by William Herbert Gropper (Milton Herbert Cropper?). Photography: Joseph Walker. Art Director: Harrison Wiley. Editor: Maurice Wright. Producer: Harry Cohn. Sound Engineers: John P. Livadary, Harry Blanchard. Assistant Director: David Selman.

Cast: Barbara Stanwyck (Kay Arnold), Ralph Graves (Jerry Strange), Lowell Sherman (Bill Standish), Marie Prevost (Dot Lamar), Nance O'Neil (Mrs. Strange), George Fawcett (Mr. Strange), Johnnie Walker (Charlie), Juliette Compton (Claire Collins).

Jerry Strange, son of a well-known railroad contractor, sets out to become an artist and converts an expensive New York penthouse into a studio. His girl friend, Claire, borrows the studio for a party that turns into a drunken orgy. When she refuses to leave with him, he takes a drive along the waterfront, where he meets Kay Arnold, who has just left a yachting party. Perceiving something in her, he engages her as a model for a painting to be called "Hope." His friend Bill Standish is discouraged by the girl and turns to her roommate. The long posing sessions bring out Kay's true self, which contrasts markedly with the wisecracking adventuress she pretends to be. Jerry proposes to Kay; but his parents forbid the marriage. Kay embarks for Havana with Bill, but, unable to continue, jumps overboard. Jerry finds her at a hospital and, convinced of her love, stays by her.

> ... stands quite alone for its amusing dialogue,
> the restrained performances of nearly all the play-
> ers and a general lightness of handling that com-
> mends the direction of Frank Capra. --The New
> York Times, May 24, 1930, p. 21.

RAIN OR SHINE. Columbia. 1930. 87 minutes.

Director: Frank Capra. Screenplay: Dorothy Howells, Jo
Swerling. Based on the play by James Gleason. Photography: Joseph Walker. Art Director: Harrison Wiley. Music: Bakaleinikoff. Songs: "Happy Days are Here Again"
and "Rain or Shine" by Jack Yellen and Milton Ager. "Sitting on a Rainbow" by Yellen and Dan Dougherty. Producer:
Harry Cohn. Editor: Maurice Wright. Sound Engineers:
John P. Livadary, Edward Bernds. Assistant Director:
Sam Nelson.

Cast: Joe Cook (Smiley), Louise Fazenda (Frankie),
Joan Peers (Mary), Dave Chasen (Dave), William Collier,
Jr. (Bud), Tom Howard (Amos), Alan Roscoe (Dalton),
Adolph Milar (Foltz), Clarence Muse (Nero), Edward Mar-
tindel (Mr. Conway), Nora Lane (Grace Conway), Tyrrell
Davis (Lord Gwynne).

Smiley Johnson, business manager for Mary Rainey,
falls in love with her and tries, against great odds, to make
a success of her father's circus. But Mary has fallen for
Bud Conway, a college boy who joined the circus for a lark.
Bud wants his father to back the circus financially, but
Smiley's ridiculous behavior at a dinner kills the project.
Mary fires him and makes Dalton, the ringmaster, manager.
He and Foltz, the lion tamer, conspire to stir up dissension
and make a profit, and the performers go on strike. But
Smiley returns and dismisses them all, putting on a one-
man show with the assistance of Bud and his friends. The
audience riots, causing a tent fire from which Bud rescues
Mary. Convinced of the sincerity of the young lovers,
Smiley exits gracefully.

> ... plenty of comedy ... much better than average
> circus picture.... --Sime, Variety, July 23, 1930.

DIRIGIBLE. Columbia. 1931. 100 minutes.

Director: Frank Capra. Screenplay: Jo Swerling, from a
story by Lt. Cdr. Frank W. Wead. Continuity: Dorothy
Howell. Photography: Joseph Walker. Aerial Photography:
Elmer Dyer. Special Effects: W. J. Butler. Editor: Maurice Wright. Producer: Harry Cohn.

Cast: Jack Holt (Bradon), Ralph Graves (Frisky
Pierce), Fay Wray (Helen Pierce), Hobart Bosworth (Louis
Rondelle), Roscoe Karns (Sock McGuire), Harold Goodwin
(Hansen), Clarence Muse (Clarence), Emmett Corrigan (Ad-
miral Martin), Alan Roscoe (Commander of the U.S.S. Lex-
ington), Selmer Jackson (Lt. Rowland).

Lieutenant Commander Jack Bradon, a U.S. Navy
pilot, champions the use of dirigibles for exploration. Lt.
Frisky Pierce, another pilot, supports the use of airplanes.
Bradon asks Pierce to accompany him on a dirigible expedi-
tion to the South Pole. But Pierce's wife, Helen, appeals
to Bradon not to take him along, and Bradon leaves without
him. Before the Los Angeles reaches the South Pole, it
buckles in a storm and is wrecked. Those aboard are res-
cued and returned to base. Before another ship can be built
for the antarctic trip, Lt. Pierce sets sail for the pole with
explorer Louis Rondelle, who was also on board the Los
Angeles. He carries a sealed letter from Helen, a letter in
which she asks for a divorce because he's away so often.
Pierce and Rondelle attempt to land a plane at the pole, but
they crash and are marooned. Radio messages bring Bradon
in a newly-constructed dirigible to rescue the party. When
they return to civilization, Bradon is greeted by public ac-
claim and Pierce by his wife.

> Ten reels of noise without a single idea. Money
> today, forgotten tomorrow.--Myles Connolly to
> Frank Capra, on DIRIGIBLE, in The Name above
> the Title, p. 129.

> ... quite interesting if you don't try to dig in.
> The story, of course, is the worst of it all....
> Graves ... organizes an expedition of his own and
> goes floppo at the pole.--Sime, Variety, April 8,
> 1931.

> ... Hollywood is incapable of delivering the goods
> in anything like a plain, objective van.... The

> keen taste of hardship and achievement is smoth-
> ered in He-Man's Relish. ... Once there were
> men who thought the earth was flat; it looks like
> a triangle to Hollywood. --Peter Fleming, on DIR-
> IGIBLE, The Spectator, June 27, 1931, p. 1007.

The MIRACLE WOMAN. Columbia. 1931. 87 minutes.

Director: Frank Capra. Screenplay: Jo Swerling. From
the play by Robert Riskin and John Meehan, "Bless You,
Sister!" Continuity: Dorothy Howell. Photography: Joseph
Walker. Editor: Maurice Wright. Producer: Harry Cohn.
Sound: Glenn Rominger.

Cast: Barbara Stanwyck (Florence Fallon), David
Manners (John Carson), Sam Hardy (Hornsby), Beryl Mercer
(Mrs. Higgins), Russell Hopton (Dan Welford), Charles Mid-
dleton (Simpson), Eddie Boland (Collins), Thelma Hill (Gus-
sie), Aileen Carlyle (Violet), Al Stewart (Brown), Harry
Todd (Briggs).

Florence "Faith" Fallon, the daughter of a minister,
blames the death of her father on his inhuman treatment by
the church elders, who forced him to resign because of old
age, and on his congregation, which was deaf to his message. Hornsby, a big-city promoter, convinces Florence
that she should capitalize on her own oratorical powers and
Biblical knowledge by starting a revival house. She agrees,
and Hornsby becomes her business manager. The temple is
packed every night. The show begins with Florence walking
down the steps above the stage to a lions' cage, opening the
door, and entering. She then delivers her message sur-
rounded by lions. One night she encounters John Carson, a
blind aviator, who was saved from suicide when he heard
one of her talks from the radio in the apartment below. His
profession of faith in the religious sham stirs her to shame.
She and Carson fall in love, which moves Hornsby to threaten
to expose her unless she goes with him to Monte Carlo.
(He will announce that they are on a pilgrimage to the Holy
Land.) Florence decides to reveal herself publicly as a
cheat and a liar at a farewell prayer meeting. But Hornsby,
attempting to darken the place, causes a short circuit in the
control box, and the tabernacle is destroyed by fire. Hornsby dies, and Florence and John escape to a happier life.

This film seems to be the source for many of the

ideas in Capra's later MEET JOHN DOE. (Robert Riskin's
name appears in the credits for both films.) The Stanwyck
role in The MIRACLE WOMAN becomes the Stanwyck and
Cooper roles in MEET JOHN DOE.

> A superior picture, if only by virtue of its two
> magnificent scenes of evangelistic mummery in a
> tabernacle, is The MIRACLE WOMAN. Here, at
> least, is some excellent and genuine material of
> life, striking in its unfamiliarity and effectively
> presented.... Its romantic motif, however, leaves
> much to be desired.--Alexander Bakshy, The Na-
> tion, September 2, 1931, p. 237.

> This is one of those wonderful films of the early
> thirties which attacked all the rotten, sacred things
> the studios could think of ... a much better exam-
> ple of [Capra's] work than DIRIGIBLE....--Richard
> Koszarski, "Lost and Found," Film Comment,
> Spring 1971, p. 71.

FORBIDDEN.   Columbia.   1932.   83 minutes.

Director: Frank Capra. Screenplay: Jo Swerling, from
Capra's story. Photography: Joseph Walker. Editor: Mau-
rice Wright. Producer: Harry Cohn. Sound: Edward
Bernds.

    Cast: Barbara Stanwyck (Lulu Smith), Adolphe Menjou
(Bob Grover), Ralph Bellamy (Al Holland), Dorothy Peterson
(Helen), Thomas Jefferson (Wilkinson), Charlotte V. Henry
(Roberta, age 18), Myrna Fresholtz (Roberta, age 2), Tom
Ricketts (Briggs), Halliwell Hobbes (florist), Flo Wix (Mrs.
Smith), Claude King (Mr. Jones), Robert Graves (Mr. Eck-
ner), Frankie Raymond, Gertrude Pedlar, Wilfred Noy.

    Lulu Smith, a small-town librarian, splurges on a
vacation to Cuba. On the steamship bound for Havana she
meets Bob Grover, a district attorney, when he mistakes
her stateroom (66) for his (99). They begin a love affair
and return together to New York, where Lulu takes a job as
reference librarian on a newspaper. There Bob confesses
that he's married, to an invalid wife whose injury he was
responsible for. She leaves him, but when she has a baby
the two are reconciled. While his wife is in Vienna, Grover
invites Lulu to live with him. Al Holland, who works with

the same paper as Lulu, is out to "get" Bob, who is rising
in politics. One day he chances upon Lulu with her child in
a park. She claims she is the governess of the girl, adopted
in Mrs. Grover's absence. She continues as "governess" at
the Grovers even after Mrs. Grover returns. Finally, unable to bear watching another woman bring up her daughter,
she returns to the paper on a lonely hearts column. Holland
is now the managing editor. Years later, Bob is nominated
for governor, but he wants to flee with Lulu and renounce
his career. She, to prevent him from throwing it away,
marries Holland. Bob is elected, but Holland unearths the
secret of his romance with Lulu and swears to break the
story. When he strikes Lulu, she shoots him and destroys
the evidence of her child's birth. Grover pardons the tired
and broken Lulu after a year in prison and dies with her at
his bedside. Her spirit gone, she wanders away down a
crowded street.

> The picture is long, too long, but is replete with
> good workmanship, some laughs, pathos, and is
> an interesting tale well played.--Sid., Variety,
> January 12, 1932.

> Absorbing love drama.--Film Daily, January 17,
> 1932.

> ... a cumbersome effort at story-telling.... It
> happens invariably when a director tackles his own
> brainchild that the result is disappointing....--
> Mordaunt Hall, The New York Times, January 11,
> 1932, p. 28.

> I had yet to learn that drama is not really just
> actors weeping and suffering all over the place....
> FORBIDDEN ended up as two hours of soggy,
> 99.44% pure soap opera.--Frank Capra, The Name
> above the Title, p. 134.

The Why We Fight series

PRELUDE TO WAR. U.S. War Department. 1942.
53 minutes.

Director: Frank Capra. Screenplay: Eric Knight, Anthony
Veiller. Music: Dimitri Tiomkin. Editor: William Hornbeck. Commentary: Walter Huston.

Manny Farber called PRELUDE TO WAR "Capra's best film, " but to me it seems inferior not just to the next two in the Why We Fight series, but to just about every Capra before it too. It tries to cover too much ground--American history and American social and political principles and the rise to power of Hitler, Mussolini, and Hirohito. It's skimpy in all areas, though when it finally focusses on the Japanese invasion of Manchuria in 1931, it begins to look like the more thoroughgoing documentaries that were to follow it. It then proceeds with the Japanese assault on Shanghai in 1932 and again lapses into vagueness and visual and verbal generalities about war and death. The unrealistically wide scope of PRELUDE TO WAR generates questionable transitions, as for instance when the scene shifts from Germany to Japan: "In Japan you'd expect things to be done a little differently. " (Why?) American ideals are conveyed in trite phrases ("On Sunday, if he felt like it, John Q went to any church he pleased"), and the enemy threat stated in the broadest, most useless terms ("Remember those faces"--Mussolini, Hitler, Hirohito--"If you ever meet them, don't hesitate. ")

> The film makes the very human mistake of holding idyllic Greenbelt to be a not uncommon American neighborhood, which is as excusable as thinking of your Sunday best as your characteristic dress. -- Manny Farber, The New Republic, May 31, 1943, p. 734.

The NAZIS STRIKE. U.S. War Department. 1942. 42 minutes.

Director: Frank Capra, Anatole Litvak. Screenplay: Eric Knight, Anthony Veiller. Music: Dimitri Tiomkin. Editor: William Hornbeck. Commentary: Walter Huston, Anthony Veiller.

The NAZIS STRIKE is a well-engineered documentation of the Nazi conquest of Europe in the Thirties. The slick engineering makes alarming the ease with which Germany took the Rhineland, Austria, Czechoslovakia, and Poland. The animation probably over-simplifies the subject, but it allows a great deal of information to be passed in a very short time. And the film's breakneck pace parallels and suggests the relentlessness of Hitler's armies. The combination of animation and live-action footage creates a

strong impression of completeness.   Long-range battle plans
plus shots of howitzers hastily dispatched across Germany
to Poland leave one beginning to identify uneasily with the
exhilaration Hitler perhaps felt in wielding his power.   The
various strategies to slice up Poland plus "reaction shots"
of the Poles and their war-ravaged cities, and one experiences the misuse of power.   You're on both sides whether
or not you want to be.

Though it was made to aid the war effort, The NAZIS
STRIKE is as much a history lesson as propaganda.   Only
when the narrator (sometimes Walter Huston, a good choice
of voice) gets tough ("stooges who fell for this bunk") does
it seem like routine propaganda.   Though the clips were
sometimes several years old even in 1942, there's a sense
of immediacy, in footage of Hitler, in the presentation of
news banners like "Germany-Russia pact?" followed by "Moscow Confirms It": for a moment it's not packaged history
but today's headlines.

The image of a burst of flying toy gliders launched
by German boys may seem rather a harmless one, but in
conjunction with the narrator's ominous tones it's evocative
of an unseen evil.   It's an ironically beautiful image of youth
indoctrination.   But for the most part, Capra's film hasn't
the magic of TRIUMPH OF THE WILL.   It's workmanlike,
smooth, commendable considering the differences in re-
sources (indicated by shots of uniformed masses from the
German documentary): Capra orchestrates pieces of film;
Leni Riefenstahl orchestrated the Nazis themselves (and
pieces of film).

DIVIDE AND CONQUER.   U.S. War Department.
1943.   58 minutes.

Directors: Frank Capra, Anatole Litvak.   Screenplay:
Anthony Veiller, Robert Heller.   Music: Dimitri Tiomkin.
Editor: William Hornbeck.   Commentary: Walter Huston,
Anthony Veiller.

The raw material of DIVIDE AND CONQUER is so
fascinating and horrifying, and there's so much of it, that
it overwhelms inanities in the narration and animation.   Even
most-likely-accurate description--"refugees used as tools of
war"--that sounds false is swept up in the rush to material.
It's hard to believe that this film is the real thing, not a

reconstruction, it seems so complete, coordinating as it does countries and strategies and counter-strategies, attacker and attacked. In effect it's omniscient. The animation lapses into silliness at times (little swastikas become termites); the force of the film makes the Nazis look almost laughably cruel occasionally; and the narration goes too far ("little Denmark") since the material stretches the bounds of credibility far enough without any editorializing. But this is more exciting and shocking than probably any war drama: There's no sidetracking into questionable "human interest" areas and no fitting of wars and battles into dramatic formulas.

The BATTLE OF BRITAIN. U.S. War Department. 1943. 54 minutes.

Supervision: Frank Capra. Director, Screenplay: Anthony Veiller. Music: Dimitri Tiomkin. Editor: William Hornbeck. Commentary: Walter Huston.

The BATTLE OF RUSSIA. U.S. War Department. 1943-44. 80 minutes.

Supervision: Frank Capra. Director: Anatole Litvak. Screenplay: Anthony Veiller, Robert Heller, Litvak. Music: Dimitri Tiomkin. Editor: William Hornbeck. Commentary: Walter Huston, Veiller.

> [The BATTLE OF RUSSIA] ... next to the tearful magnificence of The BIRTH OF A NATION is, I believe, the best and most important war film ever assembled in this country. --James Agee, Agee on Film, p. 57.

The BATTLE OF CHINA. U.S. War Department. 1944. 60 minutes.

Director: Frank Capra, Anatole Litvak. Screenplay: Eric Knight, Anthony Veiller. Music: Dimitri Tiomkin. Editor: William Hornbeck. Commentary: Walter Huston.

WAR COMES TO AMERICA. U.S. War Department. 1945. 70 minutes.

Supervision: Frank Capra. Director: Anatole Litvak.
Screenplay: Anthony Veiller. Music: Dimitri Tiomkin.
Editor: William Hornbeck. Commentary: Walter Huston.

Other War Documentaries which Capra either directed
or supervised:

> KNOW YOUR ALLY: BRITAIN. 1943 (1945?).
> KNOW YOUR ENEMY: JAPAN. 1945.
> KNOW YOUR ENEMY: GERMANY. 1945.
> TUNISIAN VICTORY. 1943 (1944? 1945?).
> The NEGRO SOLDIER IN WORLD WAR II. 1944.
> TWO DOWN, ONE TO GO. 1945.
> "Army-Navy Screen Magazine." 1943-45.
> ON TO TOKYO. 1945.

STATE OF THE UNION. MGM/Liberty Films. 1948. 124
minutes. (The WORLD AND HIS WIFE - British title).

Director, Producer: Frank Capra. Screenplay: Anthony
Veiller, Myles Connolly. Based on the Pulitzer Prize-win-
ning play by Howard Lindsay and Russel Crouse. Photogra-
phy: George J. Folsey. Musical Score: Victor Young. Art
Directors: Cedric Gibbons, Urie McCleary. Sets: Emile
Kuri, Edwin B. Willis. Editor: William Hornbeck. Special
Effects: A. Arnold Gillespie. Assistant Director: Arthur
S. Black. Costumes: Irene. Makeup: Jack Dawn. Hair
Styles: Sydney Guilaroff. Sound: Douglas Shearer. As-
sociate Producer: Veiller.

Cast: Spencer Tracy (Grant Matthews), Katharine
Hepburn (Mary Matthews), Van Johnson (Spike MacManus),
Angela Lansbury (Kay Thorndyke), Adolphe Menjou (Jim Con-
over), Lewis Stone (Sam Thorndyke), Howard Smith (Sam
Parrish), Maidel Turner (Lulubelle Alexandar[1]), Raymond
Walburn (Judge Alexandar[1]), Charles Dingle (Bill Hardy),
Florence Auer (Grace Draper), Pierre Watkin (Sen. Lauter-
back), Margaret Hamilton (Norah), Irving Bacon (Buck Swen-
son), Patti Brady (Joyce Matthews), George Nokes (Grant,
Jr.), Carl "Alfalfa" Switzer (bellboy), Tom Pedi (barber),
Tom Fadden (waiter), Charles Lane (Blink Moran), Art Baker
(Leith, radio announcer), Rhea Mitchell (Jenny), Arthur
O'Connell (first reporter), Marion Martin, Tor Johnson

---

1. Or "Alexander."

192   The Films of Frank Capra

(wrestler), Stanley Andrews (senator), Dave Willock (pilot), Russell Meeker (politician), Frank L. Clarke (Joe Crandall), David Clarke (Rusty Miller), Del Henderson (Broder), Edwin Cooper (Bradbury), Davison Clark (Crump), Francis Pierlot (Josephs), Brandon Beach (editor), Howard Mitchell and Boyd Davis (doctors), Franklyn Farnum, Maurice Cass (little man), Frank Austin (crackpot), Roger Moore (photographer), Sam Ash (editor), Mahlon Hamilton (businessman), Garry Owen (Brooklynite).

On his deathbed, newspaper magnate Sam Thorndyke leaves his daughter Kay his chain of papers, with the hope that she will use them to gain control of the Republican party. Kay and Jim Conover, a powerful Republican, set out to convince airplane manufacturer Grant Matthews that he has a chance as a dark horse candidate for the Presidential nomination. But he says that he's too busy and doesn't want the job. But, as he passes the White House, he begins to get worked up about U.S. history and soon launches himself on a campaign. Conover, to bolster Grant's chances, convinces the latter's estranged wife, Mary, to pretend that they are still happily married. When she discovers that he's having an affair with Kay, she makes him sleep on a mattress on the bedroom floor. Conover, now his campaign manager, and Kay tell Matthews that he must play ball with any politico who can deliver votes and that he must offend no one. Mary urges him not to compromise his liberal beliefs. A farm-bloc senator backs Matthews in return for the right to name the Secretary of Agriculture. A labor leader supports him in return for a say in choosing the Secretary of Labor. Matthews, however, begins to worry his backers with his campaign speeches' unconventional frankness. Mary refuses to lie for her husband in a radio speech, and Kay agrees to read it instead. Mary later relents, but Grant, realizing that he has been dishonest with the voters, publicly retires from the race.

STATE OF THE UNION has, for many years, been withdrawn from television, theatres, and 16-millimeter film rental libraries. At the time I saw it, in 1963, on television, I thought it was the best of the Hepburn-Tracy films I had seen.[1] Unfortunately, I have hardly any memory now

_____

1. It certainly can't be worse than SEA OF GRASS, KEEPER OF THE FLAME, WOMAN OF THE YEAR, and PAT AND MIKE, which are all pretty flimsy. On the other hand, I doubt that it could be better than ADAM'S RIB, which is pretty good.

of it, except of a scene in a plane, which I suspect is so
memorable less because of some special brilliance than because of the broadness of its comedy. (That is, for the
same reason that ARSENIC AND OLD LACE is so hard to
forget.) And I now flinch automatically at the mere thought
of film adaptations of "sophisticated" Broadway plays (like
The WOMEN, HOLIDAY, The MAN WHO CAME TO DINNER),
which is no fault of STATE OF THE UNION, I suppose. But
what makes me most suspicious of its reputation (with me)
are the reviews of the time--which are almost uniformly
mixed--particularly Philip T. Hartung's review in Commonweal. Hartung was one of Capra's friends among critics in
the Forties--and by "friend" I mean someone who would let
Capra know when and where he went wrong, where he went
right. I have to give his sense of disappointment in STATE
OF THE UNION as much weight as my fond non-memory of
it. I give weight to the other reviews only as they echo his
mixed feelings.

> It is surprising that Frank Capra, who knows a
> good movie when he or anyone else makes one,
> hasn't done something more cinematic with STATE
> OF THE UNION. This lively play was very amus-
> ing on the stage in spite of weaknesses in its hur-
> ried conclusion. As a movie it has become a se-
> ries of funny wisecracks statically spouted before
> the camera, and if the sound track were turned
> off, we'd have very little to see.... At times
> Capra tries to instil a little action into the clever-
> ly worded situations, but usually this action be-
> comes horseplay, as in the airplane scene that
> moves all right but is downright silly. If you don't
> mind a comedy's being stagey ... you'll get some
> gay laughs out of this lengthy film.--Philip T.
> Hartung, The Commonweal, May 7, 1948, p. 80.
>
> ... whirlwind pace.... Johnson nearly walks away
> with the picture.... Addition of flying scenes im-
> possible on stage, was a stroke of genius.... en-
> joyable film.--Variety, March 24, 1948.
>
> ... a rattling good screen comedy.--Bosley Crow-
> ther, The New York Times, May 2, 1948.
>
> ... richly entertaining ... adult, literate and in-
> telligent.--Cue, April 24, 1948.

... fast and bright entertainment.... For all its
fine points, however, it does not touch the heights
of greatness.... In transferring the wise and
witty stage comedy to the screen, Capra clearly
relied unduly on hoke and stereotyped business. --
Hollywood Reporter, March 24, 1948.

... an ancient, contrived and unlikely plot.... The
movies have a habit of making wives so much more
desirable than mistresses that only perverseness
or the need for a plot could lead a man into adult-
ery ... too predictable and too synthetic to be more
than fair.--Robert Hatch, The New Republic, May
10, 1948, p. 30.

When STATE OF THE UNION most closely follows
the Lindsay-Crouse play from which it derives, it
is a fairly enjoyable business, but when it lights
out on its own, it becomes a sad spectacle.--John
McCarten, The New Yorker, May 1, 1948, p. 83.

STATE OF THE UNION and WATCH ON THE
RHINE, The PHILADELPHIA STORY and YOU
CAN'T TAKE IT WITH YOU were first-rate screen
entertainment.--Kenneth Macgowan, Script, February, 1949, p. 36.

... [STATE OF THE UNION] is an extremely good
picture.... Frank Capra can be complimented on
capturing the atmosphere of back-stair political
life with its ... jolliness and false bonhomie, its
bustle and excitement, its illusion of power....--
Virginia Graham, The Spectator, July 30, 1948,
p. 142.

... Tracy, as in all his recent pictures, lacks
fire; Hepburn's affectation of talking like a woman
trying simultaneously to steady a loose dental brace
sharply limits her range of expression; Johnson,
playing a Drew Pearsonish columnist, is no more
effective than Pearson would be playing Johnson....
Only Lansbury ... does any real acting.... a
mildly entertaining movie.--Time, May 3, 1948,
p. 93.

Our Mr. Sun. Bell Telephone/N. W. Ayer & Son. 1954

(1956). 59 minutes. color. (aka The Sun). Shown on
CBS-TV Nov. 19, 1956.

Director, Script, Producer: Frank Capra. Source Books:
Our Sun by Donald Menzel, Energy Sources by Eugene Ayres
and Charles A. Scarlott. Photography: Harold Wellman.
Animation: UPA. Sets: Wiard Ihnen. Editor: Frank P.
Keller. Assistant Director: Arthur S. Black. Research:
Jeanne Curtis.

        Cast: Eddie Albert (fiction writer), Dr. Frank Bax-
ter (Dr. Research), Sterling Holloway, Marvin Miller, Lionel
Barrymore.

        (I probably saw Capra's science series before I saw
any of his features. I know I saw Hemo the Magnificent in
1957 and I remember seeing a lot of Frank Baxter on TV
around this time.)

        Once the "entertainment" (Dr. Baxter and Albert mak-
ing asses of themselves matching wits with an animated Mr.
Sun and Father Time) is out of the way and the film gets
down to Baxter's facts about the sun, Our Mr. Sun is bright
and even illuminating. Like PRELUDE TO WAR, its scope
is wide, but the avalanche of data, information, and descrip-
tive details has a cumulative effect--you feel that you've got-
ten a thorough introduction to the subject. For something
that at times displays a rather rudimentary (to put it mildly)
idea of what's "entertaining," Our Mr. Sun finally gets pretty involved in its subject, finally gets to be entertaining.
It's most interesting for the bifurcation of its subject into
what scientists knew (in 1954) about the sun and into what
they had yet to learn (about the corona, chlorophyll, etc.):
facts plus mystery, an irresistible combination. And it's
actually more vital today: it ends by proposing alternatives
to current energy sources and predicts a fuel crisis by 1975!

Hemo the Magnificent. Bell Telephone/N. W. Ayer & Son.
1957. 59 minutes. color. Shown on CBS-TV March 20,
1957.

Director, Script, Producer: Frank Capra. Photography:
Harold Wellman. Animation: Shamus Culhane Studios.
Musical Supervision: Raoul Kraushaar. Editor: Frank P.
Keller. Assistant Director: Arthur S. Black. Associate
Producer: Joseph Sistrom.

Cast: Dr. Frank Baxter (Dr. Research), Richard
Carlson (fiction writer), Sterling Holloway.

The Strange Case of the Cosmic Rays.   Bell Telephone/N.
W. Ayer & Son.   1957.   59 minutes.   color.   Shown on
NBC-TV October 25, 1957.

Director, Producer: Frank Capra.   Script: Capra, Jonathan
Latimer.   Animation: Shamus Culhane Studios.

Cast: Richard Carlson (fiction writer), Dr. Frank
Baxter (Dr. Research), Baird Puppets (Dostoevsky, Dickens,
Poe).

The Unchained Goddess.   Bell Telephone/N. W. Ayer & Son.
1958.   59 minutes.   color.   (aka Meteora, the Unchained
Goddess).   Shown on NBC-TV February 12, 1958.

Producer: Frank Capra.   Director: Richard Carlson.
Script: Capra, Jonathan Latimer.   Photography: Harold
Wellman.   Animation: Shamus Culhane Studios.   Musical
Supervision: Raoul Kraushaar.   Editor: Frank P. Keller.
Associate Producer: Joseph Sistrom.

Cast: Richard Carlson, Dr. Frank Baxter.

RENDEZVOUS IN SPACE.   Martin-Marietta Corp.   1964.
19 minutes.   (aka REACHING FOR THE STARS).

Director, Screenplay: Frank Capra.

A combination-live-action-and-animation short made
for the New York World's Fair.   Used in conjunction with a
live demonstration of space vehicles.

Appendix II

PERIPHERAL FILMS

EVERY MAN FOR HIMSELF. Pathe. 1924. 2 reels.
Director: Bob McGowan? Screenplay: Frank Capra. Producer: Hal Roach.
"Our Gang" comedy.

> ... introduction of a pair of twins ... one a battler and the other a pacifist. --Motion Picture News, October 18, 1924, p. 2001.

(According to Time, August 8, 1938, Capra wrote four other "Our Gang" comedies.)

The WILD GOOSE CHASER. Pathe/Sennett. 1924. 2 reels.
Director: Lloyd Bacon. Screenplay: Frank Capra, Vernon Smith?
Cast: Ben Turpin, Madeline Hurlock, Dot Farley, Jack Cooper.

OFFICIAL OFFICERS. 1925.
Screenplay: Frank Capra? Producer: Hal Roach.
"Our Gang" comedy.

SUPER-HOOPER-DYNE LIZZIES. Pathe/Sennett. 1925. 2 reels.
Director: Del Lord. Screenplay: Frank Capra, Jefferson Moffit(t).
Cast: Andy Clyde, Billy Bevan, Lillian Knight.

BREAKING THE ICE. Pathe/Sennett. 1925. 2 reels.
Screenplay: Frank Capra, Jefferson Moffit(t).
Cast: Ralph Graves, Marvin Lobach, Alice Day.

The MARRIAGE CIRCUS. Pathe/Sennett. 1925. 2 reels.
Director: Reggie Morris, Ed Kennedy. Screenplay: Frank
Capra, Vernon Smith.
     Cast: Ben Turpin, Madeline Hurlock, Louise Carver.

GOOD MORNING, NURSE! Pathe/Sennett. 1925. 2 reels.
Director: Del Lord. Screenplay: Frank Capra, Jefferson
Moffit(t).
     Cast: Ralph Graves, Olive Borden, Marvin Lobach.

CUPID'S BOOTS. Pathe/Sennett. 1925. 2 reels.
Director: Ed Kennedy. Screenplay: Frank Capra.
     Cast: Ralph Graves, Thelma Hill.

SOLDIER MAN. Pathe/Sennett. 1926. 3 reels.
Screenplay: Frank Capra?

The SWIM PRINCESS. Pathe/Sennett. 1928. 2 reels.
color.
Director: Alf Goulding. Screenplay: James Tynan, Frank
Capra. Editor: William Hornbeck.
     Cast: Daphne Pollard, Andy Clyde, Carole Lombard.

The BURGLAR. Pathe/Sennett. 1928. 2 reels. (aka
SMITH'S BURGLAR).
Director: Phil Whitman. Screenplay: Dick Barrows, Frank
Capra. Editor: William Hornbeck. Supervision: John
Waldron.
     Cast: Raymond McKee, Ruth Hiatt, Billy Gilbert.

IF YOU COULD ONLY COOK. Columbia. 1935. 70 minutes.
Director: William A. Seiter.
     Falsely advertised in England as a Frank Capra Pro-
duction.

WHEN YOU'RE IN LOVE. Columbia. 1937. 104 minutes.
     Robert Riskin's only film as director.

CAVALCADE OF ACADEMY AWARDS. Warner Brothers.

1940. 30 minutes. part color.
Supervision: Frank Capra. Director: Ira Genet. Screenplay: Owen Crump. Commentary: Carey Wilson. Photography: Charles Rosher.
    With Bette Davis.
    A history of the Academy of Motion Picture Arts and
Sciences from 1928 to 1939.

SULLIVAN'S TRAVELS. Paramount. 1941. 91 minutes.
Director: Preston Sturges.

    Sullivan: "I wanted to make you something outstand-
ing ... something that would realize the potentialities of
film as the sociological and artistic medium that it is ...
with a little sex in it. Something like...."
    Studio executive: "Something like Capra. I know."

EVE KNEW HER APPLES. Columbia. 1945. 64 minutes.
Director: Will Jason. Screenplay: E. Edwin Moran, from
a story by Rian James. Unofficial remake of IT HAPPENED
ONE NIGHT.
    Cast: Ann Miller, William Wright, Robert Williams.

    A newspaperman mistakes a vacationing radio star
for an escaped murderess.

        On stage and off, sitting in a bus, lying on a hay-
        stack ... Miss Miller does four songs. --Variety,
        April 25, 1945.

MAGIC TOWN. RKO/Riskin. 1947. 103 minutes.
Director: William Wellman. Screenplay: Robert Riskin.
    Cast: James Stewart, Jane Wyman, Ned Sparks.

        MAGIC TOWN, directed by William A. Wellman,
        has provoked everywhere damp murmurs of 'Cap-
        ra!' and as one who has never appreciated Capra
        I find the insult well merited. This mixture of
        well-starred sentimentality and politics (or pa-
        triotics) seems to me quite unexportable. Its first
        half-hour entertains, when a public poll expert
        (James Stewart) finds the small town to provide
        him with an unerring sample of national opinion,
        but after that we have to slop through ... a good

> deal of jubilation about the wonderfulness of peo-
> ple.--William Whitebait, New Statesman and Na-
> tion, August 13, 1949.

MAGIC TOWN is Capra material so clumsily handled
that it's not just hard to say where it went wrong--it's hard
to say where it could possibly have gone right. The premise
is cursorily established--its importance is assumed rather
than demonstrated. And that premise, rather than logically
developed, is just added to piecemeal. The dialogue, apparently in the hope of making Stewart out a good-bad guy,
variously describes him as a "dreamer" and a "city slicker,"
but he in fact seems a rather neutral figure dramatically,
just an enterprising businessman. And, astonishingly, the
script lifts almost intact the scene from MEET JOHN DOE
(the film's closest antecedent) in which Regis Toomey and
Ann Doran represent the John Does--the couple here represent what can at best be only vaguely described as Public-
Minded Citizens--and the couple are played by Regis Toomey
and Ann Doran!

GOOD SAM. RKO. 1948. 113 minutes.
Director, Producer: Leo McCarey.

> In the role of the hero, Gary Cooper does a sub-
> limely indifferent job of kidding every do-gooder
> that he has played since Mr. Deeds, plus a couple
> of memorable do-gooders that Jimmy Stewart has
> played.--Bosley Crowther, The New York Times,
> September 17, 1948, p. 28.

WESTWARD THE WOMEN. MGM. 1951. 116 minutes.
Director: William A. Wellman. Screenplay: Charles
Schnee, from a story, "Pioneer Woman," by Frank Capra.

WESTWARD THE WOMEN is notable for its re-
strained, almost documentary-like presentation of wildly implausible material, a wagon-train trip by women to wife-
hungry men in the West. The sound track is dominated not
by music but by the sounds of wind and wagon wheels, and
most of the cast underplays admirably. Unfortunately, the
material is not just implausible, but uninteresting--Wellman's
direction only makes it more plausible, not more interesting.

SHANGRI-LA. A Kevin Duffy Production. c1972. 80 minutes.

> Search for lost horizons in the real Himalayas. --
> Budget Films New Releases, 1973, p. 2.

Appendix III

OSCARS AND OSCAR NOMINATIONS

LADY FOR A DAY
      Nominations:
          Best Actress (May Robson)
          Directing
          Best Picture
          Writing - Adaptation (Robert Riskin)

IT HAPPENED ONE NIGHT
      Awards:
          Best Actor (Clark Gable)
          Best Actress (Claudette Colbert)
          Directing
          Best Picture
          Writing - Adaptation (Robert Riskin)

MR. DEEDS GOES TO TOWN
      Award:
          Directing
      Nominations:
          Best Actor (Gary Cooper)
          Best Picture
          Sound Recording
          Writing - Screenplay (Robert Riskin)

LOST HORIZON
      Awards:
          Art Direction
          Film Editing
      Nominations:
          Supporting Actor (H. B. Warner)
          Assistant Director
          Music - Best Score (Dimitri Tiomkin)
          Best Picture
          Sound Recording

YOU CAN'T TAKE IT WITH YOU
 Awards:
  Directing
  Best Picture
 Nominations:
  Supporting Actress (Spring Byington)
  Cinematography
  Film Editing
  Sound Recording
  Writing - Screenplay (Robert Riskin)

MR. SMITH GOES TO WASHINGTON
 Award:
  Writing - Original Story (Lewis R. Foster)
 Nominations:
  Best Actor (James Stewart)
  Supporting Actor (Harry Carey)
  Supporting Actor (Claude Rains)
  Art Direction
  Directing
  Film Editing
  Music - Best Score (Dimitri Tiomkin)
  Best Picture
  Sound
  Writing - Screenplay (Sidney Buchman)

MEET JOHN DOE
 Nomination:
  Writing - Original Story (Richard Connell, Robert
   Presnell)

PRELUDE TO WAR
 Award:
  Best Documentary[1]

BATTLE OF RUSSIA
 Nomination:
  Best Documentary

IT'S A WONDERFUL LIFE
 Nominations:
  Best Actor (James Stewart)
  Directing
  Film Editing

---

1. Joint winner along with BATTLE OF MIDWAY, KOKODA
FRONT LINE, and MOSCOW STRIKES BACK.

Best Picture
Sound Recording

HERE COMES THE GROOM
 Award:
  Music - Song ("In the Cool, Cool, Cool of the
   Evening")
 Nomination:
  Writing - Motion Picture Story (Robert Riskin,
   Liam O'Brien)

A HOLE IN THE HEAD
 Award:
  Music - Song ("High Hopes")

POCKETFUL OF MIRACLES
 Nominations:
  Supporting Actor (Peter Falk)
  Costume Design - Color
  Music - Song ("Pocketful of Miracles")

Appendix IV

THE NAME ABOVE THE TITLE

Capra, Frank. <u>The Name above the Title</u>. New York:
The Macmillan Co., June, 1971, 513 pages; paperback edi-
tion: New York: Bantam Books, Inc., June, 1972, 562
pages.

 <u>The Name above the Title</u> is 500 pages of anecdotes.
The operative phrase is "500 pages." It pretty well sums
up the limitations of Capra's autobiography. It's one thing
to tell a story at such length and another for someone to
tell 500 loosely-organized pages worth of stories, fact or
fiction. Capra's book is amiable, a bit preachy, usually
fairly interesting, ultimately insubstantial for its length.

 Capra the man comes through better than Capra the
writer. He inspires the feeling that you can take him (bar-
ring failings of memory) at his word. He often sees two
sides to his stories; in fact he sometimes seems to be a bit
mechanically scrupulous in apportioning blame and credit to
himself and others, as if he were simply fulfilling an obliga-
tion to posterity. But the book's real message is that Capra
believed in what he was doing.

 In the most interesting of the scattered negative reviews of the book, Elliott Stein[1] inadvertently hit upon the
one real strength of the book. To him it's "doubly distressing: for what it does not reveal about the work, for what it
does about the man." As Pauline Kael has pointed out, no
director is to be trusted on the subject of his own work; but
what interviews, lectures, question-and-answer sessions, and
autobiographies can do is reveal the person behind the work.
Stein dismisses this quality of revelation by finding Capra's
personality ("preternatural ego") distressing. I find the revelation to be oddly fulfilling.

Partly I think because art and artists often operate through indirection and irony, we mistrust those artists who are more direct, clear. We think they must be hiding something. But in reading The Name above the Title, I was struck by Capra's conception of his career as an expression of those ideals he preached in his movies. He dedicated his talents--more nakedly than most artists; more nakedly than necessary, I think--to his fellow man, and it makes sometimes silly but somehow satisfying reading, as if you were to find out that MR. SMITH GOES TO WASHINGTON was a true story.

Unfortunately, the book is, in Stein's words, "written in a style which would do no great credit to Variety's dustbin." For instance, a verbal brawl between Alexander Korda and David O. Selznick is "really a titanic tilt of the tonsils." Or, "Yep ... he could be cast as a sad-eyed Oakie." (He means Oklahoma, though, not Jack.) Capra seems to be too eager to zip back through everything he can remember about his life (which is quite a bit)--as if by slowing down, his memories would evaporate--to bother to take much care with how well he writes. He sacrifices literary for historical value, which in the long run may turn out to have been the right thing to do. One hundred years from now we'll have a more-crudely-written but also more complete record of the life of Frank Capra. Without the literary finish, though, Capra is, ironically, tough reading. Five hundred pages of him reads like fifteen hundred of Dostoevsky. He's unhealthily dependent on the strength of the subject, the story at hand, and the stories are of widely varying quality.

The book at first gives the impression that Capra's memory is hazy, dim, and the text amounts to random recollections, comments, surmises, facts, loosely strung together and difficult to get through. As E. M. Forster writes of the alleged charm of "little things" in Jane Austen's letters: "But the little things must hold out their little hands to one another; and here there is a scrappiness which prevents even tartness from telling.... the letters lack direction."[2] In Capra's book, the little things are not always tart, and however difficult it may be to imagine a Capra work lacking "direction" (in any sense of the word), much of the book does. It carries the old Capra message--"hang in there!"--but without the art, the form, the drive of his best movies, the message is left naked and alone, all-dependent on your willingness to accept it. Philosophical pep-talks punctuate the book and even end it, but Capra's presentation of his ideals is static, as simple as the ideals themselves.

As Capra's story moves into the mid-Thirties, the anecdotes begin to get longer: they develop, there's some connective tissue to carry you through. Capra's storytelling ability seems to improve as his stories lengthen, as his memory perhaps brings things more clearly into focus, and the stories cease to seem the remembered fragments of unremembered longer stories. The lively tales of the fake-Capra film, IF YOU COULD ONLY COOK, and of the casting and making of IT HAPPENED ONE NIGHT are nice and long. They're more stories than sets of incidents related only by the fact that they're located under the same chapter head.

Their charm and readability lie primarily in their pitting of Capra against quirky adversity: "He's up! He's down! No, he's up again!" But a problem even in the more engrossing portions of the book is the reconstructed dialogue. It's sometimes unreadable, at best serviceable. It often seems to be a tin-eared transliteration of what Capra remembers people saying into the way he thinks they said it. People talk on and on, but you get little or no idea of how they talked. You never really get an idea of what Capra sounds like when he's talking, and he has a lot of dialogue. (I've heard that when Capra reads or tells these stories to audiences they're more enthralling.) The book at times reads like a script, and as badly: voiceless, toneless dialogue interspersed with stage directions.

Notes

1. "Capra Counts His Oscars," Sight and Sound, Summer 1972, pp. 162-164, a nasty look directed more at Capra's later films than at his book. Several of the factual errors that Stein cites are corrected in the paperback version: "IVAN THE TERRIBLE" is now "BEHZIN MEADOW"; "Mary Astor" is now "Gertrude Astor." (But the index persists with "Mary Astor.")

2. Abinger Harvest (New York, 1964), pp. 160-1.

INDEX